SERIOUS Training for SERIOUS Athletes

Rob Sleamaker, MS

Leisure Press
Champaign, Illinois

Developmental Editor: Sue Ingels Mauck
Copyeditor: David Dobbs
Proofreader: Peter Nelson
Assistant Editors: Robert King, Holly Gilly
Production Director: Ernie Noa
Typesetters: Cindy Pritchard and Angela Snyder
Text Design: Keith Blomberg
Text Layout: Kimberlie Henris
Cover Design: Jack Davis
Cover Photo: ALLSPORT/Vandystadt
Interior Photos: Alan Jakubek, Kimberlie Henris, Ernie Noa
Illustrations By: Tim Offenstein
Printed By: Versa Press

ISBN: 0-88011-338-3

Library of Congress Cataloging-in-Publication Data

Sleamaker, Rob, 1957-
    Serious training for serious athletes / Rob Sleamaker.
        p.   cm.
    Bibliography: p.
    Includes index.
    ISBN 0-88011-338-3
    1. Endurance sports--Training.   2. Endurance sports--Physiological
aspects.   I. Title.
GV749.5.S53   1989   88-25180
613.7'1--dc19   CIP

Printed in the United States of America

10 9 8 7 6 5 4 3 2 1

Leisure Press
A Division of Human Kinetics Publishers, Inc.
Box 5076, Champaign, IL 61820
1-800-342-5457
1-800-334-3665 (in Illinois)

To Jane Burnett—my mother, my friend, and my inspiration to meet the challenges of life with willingness, honesty, and joy.

CONTENTS

Chapter 10 Restoration as an Integral Part of the Training Process

Chapter 11 Putting It All Together: Skills for Effective Training Management

FOREWORD

I n *SERIOUS Training for Serious Athletes*, Rob Sleamaker shares invaluable ideas and information on precisely planning and programming your training and, more important, on dissecting and evaluating your routine as the year progresses. His structured program is different from the scores of other available athletic training regimens because it can be designed completely by you and is adaptable to the daily stresses or changes you may encounter. As Rob states, "The training plan is only as good as the work that goes into creating, maintaining, and adjusting it."

Seldom do I read through a book with notepad in hand, but the wealth of information here will motivate you to do just that. *SERIOUS Training for Serious Athletes* describes in detail a day-by-day, progressive training program. The highest hurdle in structuring the program to make it your own is to objectively critique your past training habits. Rob makes it easy to collect important information about your training background, goals, and objectives, and he helps you use what you learn to design a concise yearly training and racing outline.

We all ask the same questions: Do I follow a hard or an easy training format? What constitutes a hard day—speed work, time trialing, training at an aerobic threshold, or all three? Should I take a day off? How should my training change during the competitive season? Do I include more race/pace, intervals, or overdistance training? *SERIOUS Training for Serious Athletes* discusses these questions thoroughly and also gives definitive answers about your specific sport and program.

I am continually reading books on physiology, exercise performance, and training methods, always hoping to get an edge on my competitors by extracting new ideas to implement in my own triathlon training program. Usually each book gives me a few tips, but not *SERIOUS Training for Serious Athletes*—there I found endless information! Let me highlight just a few of the helpful ideas:

Rob defines "systematic training" and training cycles during the year. Most athletes and coaches continue to overload the body until failure is reached, without looking for a recovery cycle to rejuvenate physically and psychologically. Using the concept of a monthly "periodization cycle," you learn to chart your progress by a "stair-stepping" program, allowing your body to recover every fourth week from the previous three weeks of strenuous exercise. Rob explains the physiology and psychology that underlie the premise for this format and provides an extremely helpful process for reevaluating the plateaus you may experience during a year-round training program.

Regardless of your training experience, you can use the concept of periodization effectively to establish parameters for each training stage. Rob describes numerous examples of endurance sports to which the periodization system can be applied; it works whether your goal is a 5K run, a 30K cross-country ski event, or an Ironman triathlon.

Rob's in-depth discussion of training variables not only defines the different types of training and the related physiology, but also helps you translate that information into your own training regimen. Complex physiology is described in layperson's language and is applied to the systematic training procedures with numerous examples.

The book climaxes with a personalized program that can be structured down to the last minute of a workout, yet offers variety and fluctuation for those who desire them. By teaching you to evaluate your training program critically and create a personal worksheet, *SERIOUS Training for Serious Athletes* offers you a fantastic tool for overcoming training staleness and increasing your motivation.

Whether your aspirations are to pursue endurance sports at the local level or to become a world champion, *SERIOUS Training for Serious Athletes* is a marvelous resource for analyzing, evaluating, and critiquing your training program. The book is a must for the serious endurance athlete. I am certainly fortunate to have read it months before my competitors will have access to it.

Dave Scott
Davis, California

PREFACE

A s a sport physiologist, researcher, coach, athlete, and writer, I have devoted my career to a scientific approach to training, both for endurance athletes and for people who simply want to get the most out of their fitness training. Since 1980 I've worked with elite runners, skiers, cyclists, triathletes, and biathletes. It wasn't long before I observed that some athletes trained more intelligently and effectively than others. This was particularly true for athletes trained in Scandinavia, Germany, the Eastern Bloc countries, and New Zealand, and for athletes coached in America with those same foreign methods.

I owe my initial pursuit of the secrets behind these athletes' success to my friend Peter Hoag, a two-time Olympian in the biathlon. In the summer of 1984, he and I spent a lot of time together training and discussing ideas about training. I spent much of this time taking notes, timing Peter's intervals, checking his pulse, mapping out his training plan with him, and doing a lot of talking about how foreign athletes trained. Peter's inquisitive nature and tremendous drive to learn inspired me to research the training methods used by the most successful athletes in the world.

I learned that many factors contributed to their success. The countries from which these athletes came usually had a large athlete base, substantial financial support for top athletes, and strong grass-roots development programs. However, with regard to training, one common thread seemed to be integral to these successful programs. That thread was systematic planning and management of training, which was apparent at all levels of development—from grade-school-age children to elite athletes.

It has been my observation that developing a training program from bits and pieces of information gathered from magazines, books, lectures, and experience can be confusing and can result in incomplete training. A systematic approach clearly seems more effective because it follows a logical, easy-to-understand method that plans daily training, tells you which activity is best to use, how to do it, what intensity to use, and how to keep track of what you actually do.

It also occurred to me that athletes and coaches at any level needed a way to integrate useful scientific and technological developments into their training plans. The systematic approach to training described in this book allows this to occur within a flexible yet well-defined structure.

I have two goals for this book. First, I want to provide you as athletes (whether recreational or competitive) with a complete, up-to-date system for understanding the concepts of physiology and with methods for planning, implementing, and monitoring your training. Second, I hope that after learning the basic concepts of systematic training, you will seek out ways to adapt this system to your own circumstances and that you will gain the skills to do so in a logical, scientifically sound manner.

How to Use This Book

Each chapter of this book relates consistently to all the others, so that the information presented may be used as a complete system of training. In chapters 1 and 2, you'll learn the basics of creating a training plan using the systematic approach. Designing a training plan involves viewing the year in terms of training cycles, assigning a percentage of the year's total training volume to each cycle, and developing proper progression in the weekly patterns within each cycle. In chapter 3 the physiological principles of training for endurance sports will be reviewed. Chapter 4 delves into the concept of training intensity. You'll learn how to monitor your training intensity using heart rate and subjective feelings. In chapters 5 and 6, you'll learn about the SERIOUS system, a model systematic training program that will help you understand how the various components of training fit into a systematic plan.

Training logs and journals are an integral part of successful systematic training. Chapter 7 discusses the many benefits of a well-kept log or journal. A log format is presented, with critical components listed. You will learn the fundamental aspects of effective log keeping and how this can help you monitor and modify training as an ongoing process.

Chapter 8 is devoted to proper warm-up, stretching, and cooldown as they relate to performance in endurance sports. Next, nutrition and fluid considerations are presented in chapter 9. You'll learn which foods supply endurance-sports "fuel." Integrating food and fluid intake with the energy demands of the training plan is a critical element of this chapter. In chapter 10 you'll discover how to include proper recovery and restoration as an integral part of the training plan. Various techniques and methods are presented, including advice on varying training loads and building in periods of rest. Finally, in chapter 11 skills for managing training effectively are reviewed. You'll learn effective use of training aids, a commonsense approach to race days, and strategies for making positive adjustments in the training plan.

Reaching Your Potential

The number of individuals involved in endurance sports is rapidly growing, and the characteristics of this group are changing. Some are interested in international competition. Others are after personal development, challenge, and variety through sports. Still others are interested in peak fitness and health and find that endurance sports offer the benefits of cardiovascular fitness, strength, and flexibility. Regardless of your goals, you will follow a plan—it's just that some people decide what their plan is 5 minutes before they walk out the door for the workout. The systematic approach outlined in this book will help you organize your goals and objectives and guide you in planning a training program that will help you reach those goals.

ACKNOWLEDGMENTS

T he process by which I have collected the information to write this book leaves me grateful to many people. In particular, I thank Peter Hoag for stimulating my intellect and curiosity to investigate better ways to train for endurance sports. Also, I am grateful to the athletes of the U.S. Biathlon Team; Jack Murray and members of the U.S. Biathlon Team Sports Medicine Council; and scientists, physicians, and coaches throughout the world who shared their information, experiences, and ideas.

I also want to thank Les Leggett for encouraging me to "go for it, because if you don't, one day you'll regret it" and Jim Clapp for teaching me the importance of honesty with one's self and love for one's work. Thanks go to Ned Frederick for his support and genius; to Bud Symmes for his great sense of direction and friendship; to Sigvart Bjontegaard, Lyle Nelson, Willie Carow, Skip Hamilton, and Tim Dahlberg for their friendship and feedback; to Jack Wilmore for helping me "learn to walk" with his firm but gentle guidance; to Donna Mae Miller for teaching me the fundamentals of philosophy and for being one of the best examples of a human being I know; to Paula Kneeland for her friendship and modeling; to Alan Jakubek for his fine photography; to Sue Mauck of Human Kinetics for her kindly manner and excellent editorial skills; to Debbie and Steve for providing the best writing environment a person could want; to Jim Miller and Pat Bannerman for their support; to Carly Geer for her expert review of the nutrition chapter; and to all the athletes I have worked with—the pleasure has been all mine. And finally, thanks to my friends and family, who have supported me as I walk along my path in life.

Rob Sleamaker
Williston, Vermont

CHAPTER

1

WHY USE THE SYSTEMATIC APPROACH TO TRAINING?

M y eyes were wide and my mouth agape. On the floor before us lay a dozen neatly kept booklets, complete with foldouts and multicolored graphs. Sigvart Bjontegaard, head coach of the U.S. biathlon team and former Norwegian national champion biathlete, explained that he had kept these training logs since he was a teenager (Figure 1.1). As we perused each graph, he pointed out aspects of each year, including his best performances, what he had learned by trying new types of training and increases in training time, and so on.

The Norwegian Ski Federation had supplied the log books, while his coaches had worked with him to develop a training program for each year. He had grown up in a culture that regarded cross-country skiing as natural part of life, as important to one's development as school, religion, and politics. These logs represented the planning, testing, data collecting, and learning common to every competitive Norwegian cross-country ski racer. Sigvart had become a master at planning and evaluating his own training programs, thanks to the structure and education offered by the training system he had been exposed to from an early age.

Since 1977 I have studied and observed training programs and methods used by both foreign and American coaches and athletes.

Figure 1.1 U.S. Olympic biathlon coach, Sigvart Bjontegaard (left), and the author review the log books and performance graphs Bjontegaard meticulously kept during his 12 years of competing at the National level in Norway.

There are many ways to plan and implement training programs for endurance sports, but they are not all equal. Many athletes and coaches believe and use nearly everything they hear or read, an approach that can be confusing and frustrating. I frequently observe athletes and coaches using approaches that seem haphazard and incomplete, with little continuity between one training year and another. Often one training plan is created for an entire team, everyone using the same times, intensities, and activities each week with complete disregard for individual differences.

The Training Language Barrier

Training has a language of its own. Like all spoken languages, this language comprises hundreds of different "dialects," each with its own nuances and connotations for commonly used training expressions. Not surprisingly, we sometimes misunderstand each other when we talk about training. For example, some coaches use the term *speed work* to refer to several types of training with varying time and intensity, including short, 8-second speed bursts, 5-minute intervals, and race/pace sessions. Another person might have a different meaning for *speed work*, such as 200-meter leg-speed drills. The examples are endless.

When an athlete attends a camp or clinic and starts working with a new coach, the training language barrier can become a serious problem. The athlete must spend valuable energy and time trying to interpret the training dialect used at the clinic, slowing the learning process considerably. Just think how fast athletes could learn if everyone spoke the same training language

In Scandinavia, Germany, and the Soviet Union, coaches are highly trained in physiology, psychology, biomechanics, and other sport sciences. Typically there is a national system used for training, and the terminology is the same across the board, both within each sport and from sport to sport. This makes it is easy for a cross-country skier to communicate with and learn from a runner, because both speak the same training language. Young children growing up with this system accelerate their learning and quickly master the skills of training for their sports. This *systematic* approach to training serves as a great translator and a universal approach that provides a foundation from which any training plan may be created.

My goal here is to share with you some information about the various components of training for endurance sports and to present the basic methods for using a systematic approach to training. But first, let's discuss your needs and goals for using this book and the systematic approach to training.

Different Athletes, Different Needs

The information presented in this book applies to a variety of endurance sports. The systematic approach to training works equally well for the beginner and the elite athlete. The principles in each instance are the same, though the content of the actual training plans will be different to suit the individuals.

Beginners will find an easy-to-follow, step-by-step approach to determining their abilities and goals and forming a training system that makes sense and that will serve as a springboard for improved fitness and success in endurance sports.

People who train to improve or maintain physical and mental health through cross-training will find the systematic approach helpful for coaxing their bodies toward greater states of fitness in a safe and sensible fashion. A foundation for mastering many aspects of conditioning can be formed through systematic training.

More advanced amateur competitors will use the systematic approach to clearly map out their progression of training and competition during the months ahead, incorporating previous experiences and training knowledge within the plan.

Serious, elite-level endurance athletes will also benefit from the systematic approach to training, which meets their need to project progressive improvements in performance over a number of years or competitive seasons. Every detail can be planned with this method, from daily workouts to training camps to national championship competitions. The elite athlete can use the systematic approach to plan and control an overall program, making sure it truly fits individual needs and circumstances.

Coaches can easily insert their own training experiences and philosophies into the systematic approach, producing an organized, efficient, manageable program for athletes. Each athlete's individual needs can be considered and met, while the integrity of the overall training program is maintained. In this way the coach can nurture each athlete's progress with detail and precision while directing the progress of the collective team. New training theories and ideas, which continually challenge the coach, can be tested and applied within the systematic approach, and the effects of each can be measured accurately.

What Is Systematic Training?

One dictionary's definition of systematic is ''being, forming, or formulated as a system, which is a regular method or order; methodical in performance.'' I define systematic training as the creation of a training framework grounded on sound physiological and psychological principles, training that allows sensible variations within that framework. As I reviewed training plans of endurance athletes from Scandinavia, Germany, the Soviet Union, and New Zealand, I found the systematic approach of each of these programs provided a foundation and a framework from which any training plan could be created. Perhaps as important, it was possible to monitor both progress in training and the stress associated with that progress.

How do you currently plan your training? Do you map out 6 to 12 months of training in advance, projecting a peak and a competition period? How do you keep up with the latest training information and incorporate it into your plan? Do you plan and train by feel?

How do you monitor the progress of your training and the stress and recovery associated with it? Does your training plan raise your conditioning level at the rate you desire?

A systematic training plan provides a reasonable format for answering these questions so that you can truly know where your training is going, why you are doing it in a given manner, and whether or not it is actually working for you.

Benefits of Training the Systematic Way

Systematic training provides several benefits.

Concise Plan

The first benefit is actually the end result of creating a systematic plan—that is, a concise, easy-to-follow training regimen that outlines each day's workout objectives, the activity to be used, the intensity of the workout, and the actual length of time of the training session. Once the regimen is created, there are none of the usual daily questions about what to do and how hard to train. Such details are worked out in advance.

Sound Principles of Sport Science

An athlete realizes the most benefit if training applies principles that lead to increased overall work capacity and fitness while maintaining good physical and psychological health. Systematic training provides a unique "checks and balances" format to accomplish this.

One Complete System

Systematic training plans map out the entire year, using distinct training cycles with their own physiological "personalities." Daily, weekly, and monthly training is planned and easily monitored for progress, recovery, and stress from training.

Adjustable Features

Once the plan is created, changes or adjustments can be easily implemented. Total training time per year can be increased or decreased without disrupting the integrity of the overall plan. Monthly cycle training volume can be adjusted and the effects easily seen and accounted for by adjusting the other months. Progress from year to year can be monitored, and the plan can be changed to make necessary adjustments. In short, with a systematic plan, any adjustment will affect the overall plan, yet such changes and their effects will be clear and easy to account for.

Opportunity to Learn From the Plan

Creating a systematic training plan provides a format from which you can learn much about the way you previously trained and to which you can apply current information about training. Systematic planning enables you to clearly identify strengths and weaknesses and develop strategies for improving those areas. The process of creating, implementing, and logging your own training plan affords you a special insight to your body's response to training. After all, it's the process rather than the final race result that leads to the greatest personal growth and development, which in turn may be applied to other aspects of life.

Variety and Motivation

A systematic training plan allows for tremendous variety in workouts if you plan it that way. Because of the variety and the fact that you created the plan, your motivation to carry it through is likely to be higher.

Planned Recovery and Injury Watchdog

The weekly pattern of the planned program allows you to plan recovery from training. Also, injuries, handicaps, or such logistical considerations as available facilities and work schedules can be accounted for in the plan.

Integration of Personal Training Philosophy

The systematic plan, because of its flexible structure, allows for the individuality of your or your coach's experiences, theories, and philosophy of training and competition.

A Training Approach That Works

The systematic approach has proven successful for athletes and coaches of many countries. This comprehensive method works equally well for endurance athletes of all levels, from the beginner to the elite athlete. There are many benefits to training the systematic way, including variety, complete planning, adjustability, and regard for individual needs and differences. The structure provides a framework around which a sound, physiologically correct plan can be created. Perhaps most importantly, systematic training serves as a universal translator so that you and coaches can begin speaking the same training language, thereby accelerating the learning process and increasing your potential to learn from other sports. If you know how long a workout is, its intensity, and the activity used, you will have a good idea of the physiological value of the workout and be able to relate it to your previous experiences.

No matter how you slice it, you (and every other athlete) follow some plan. Sometimes that plan is decided upon 5 minutes before you run out the door, with little regard for what was done yesterday and what will be done tomorrow. Sometimes a coach's plan is made up on Monday to include the rest of the week's workouts, yet is pretty much the same week after week and is used for each athlete on the team, regardless of individual differences.

I extend a personal challenge to you: Read this book and learn about systematic training. Create a systematic training plan for yourself or for the athletes you coach. If you are a coach, teach your athletes how the system works and how to design their own programs. Whether working alone or with others, keep accurate records of what you plan and the training that actually occurs as a result of the planning. If you do these things, you'll discover the types of training that are best for you and, ultimately, the most successful, come race day. As one experienced cyclist and cross-country skier who was a newcomer to systematic training remarked, ''After only 3 weeks of following the systematic training plan, I realized the approach I had previously been using was seriously flawed. . . . I actually look forward to making entries in the training log each day.''

COMPONENTS OF SYSTEMATIC TRAINING

N early everything we do follows a map of sorts. If we were all given the same destination on a map and told to go there, the approach, course, and time would vary between us. Some would carefully chart their course, using the most direct route, asking others for information about the best roads, and tuning the car for the best operating conditions. Others might select roads as they traveled, sometimes retracing their path because of a missed turn or even running out of fuel due to poor planning, and perhaps arriving late at the chosen destination. We may follow similar patterns when planning training programs. The final objective may be improved fitness and fun participation, or perhaps world-class ranking in sport. The paths we take ultimately determine our success in achieving these objectives (Figure 2.1).

Training may be regarded as a tool that, when used correctly, elicits specific physiological and psychological responses. Endurance athletes, perhaps more than other athletes, need individualized training plans that attempt to meet the specific goals of the athlete within the general guidelines for success in a given sport. The object is to improve the body's ability to supply energy to the muscles, increase energy reserves, strengthen the muscles used in the sport, and become more efficient in the specific neuromuscular functions needed in the sport. Systematic planning provides an effective, objective method whereby your coach and you can incorporate personal experiences, current scientific research results, up-to-date coaching practices, and

Figure 2.1 A training plan is like a map. It's a good idea to discuss your planned route with someone who has "been there."

innovative ideas into a structured plan. Once such a plan is created, accurate records are maintained to compare the plan with the actual training that occurs. This way, changes from month to month and year to year can be made with informed reference to the original plan and with regard to those components that worked well and those that need improvement. The plan covers a full year, including each competitive phase if there is more than one season per year.

This chapter will help you outline the objectives of a 1- to 4-year plan and learn the fundamental structure for creating a systematic training plan. The specifics of actually creating your own systematic training plan are outlined in a worksheet format in chapter 6.

Plan Objectives

Depending on your sport and level of commitment, the objectives of your plan may be outlined for 1 year or as many as 4 years (see Table

2.1). There are six basic categories to consider for the overall outline.

The first category is performance. Actual race times and ranking classifications will be identified for the events in which you are to compete. It is important to be realistic about these goals.

The second category is physical training preparation. A clear assessment of current physical strengths and weaknesses and a knowledge of proper physiological progressions is necessary for correctly mapping the objectives for this category. For example, an endurance athlete will need to develop a good aerobic endurance capacity over a period of several months before it is high enough to provide the foundation for safe and effective anaerobic capacity.

Psychological preparation is the third category. An assessment must be made to determine psychological skills and areas needing work. Then the objectives for improving these areas and for sharpening skills can be outlined.

Fourth is technical preparation. This will include learning correct body position, efficient stride, and so on, according to the requirements of the sport.

The fifth category is tactical preparation. This primarily involves race strategies.

Finally, objectives for tests and standards will be outlined. Throughout the training year, various performance objectives will serve as benchmarks for comparison to actual performance, thereby letting you check the effectiveness of the training plan on a periodic basis.

The material in this book deals primarily with physical preparation. However, a systematic training plan also provides the basic structure from which the other categories of preparation may be implemented and measured.

The Training Year

In systematic training the year is considered in terms of 52 training weeks. The type of training that occurs during each of these weeks depends on the number of competitive seasons and sports as well as when these are planned. For example, cross-country ski racers typically compete from December to March. At the elite level, these athletes do not compete in races and usually refrain from racing in other sports at a serious competitive level during the summer months. In comparison, citizen-level skiers may also compete seriously in another sport during the summer, such as running, cycling, or the triathlon. Cyclists and triathletes typically compete in racing from as early as March through October. Runners often train for a spring marathon or 10K race, then for a fall racing season as well. Regardless of how

Table 2.1
Planning Four-Year Training Objectives

ATHLETE: ___RHS___   EVENT: ___10K___

	Objectives	
	Year 1	Year 2
Performance (time)	35:20	35:00
Physical preparation	Develop general physical preparation	Improve general physical preparation
	Develop aerobic endurance	Develop muscular endurance
		Improve aerobic endurance
		Develop anaerobic endurance
Psychological preparation	Develop mental awareness and the resulting consequences	Develop mental awareness
	Attempt to modify the above	Develop self-concept
Technical preparation	Correct arm carriage	Efficient stride length
	Correct position of head	Minimum vertical bouncing
Tactical preparation	Steady pace throughout the race	Fast start in the first 400 meters
		Steady pace in the body of the race
Test and standards	$\dot{V}O_2$max = 3.7 liters	$\dot{V}O_2$max = 3.7 liters

Objectives	
Year 3	Year 4
34:30	34:00
Improve specific physical preparation	Perfect specific physical preparation
Improve muscular endurance	Perfect aerobic endurance
Perfect aerobic endurance	Perfect anaerobic endurance
Improve anaerobic endurance	
Identify anxieties and stressors and how to handle them	Identify anxieties and stressors and how to handle them
Relaxation techniques	Relaxation techniques
Relaxed running	Relaxed running
Efficient technical movement	Efficient technical movement
Take a good position before the finish	Cope with various strategies
Perfect the start	Perfect the finish
$\dot{V}O_2max = 4.1$ liters	$\dot{V}O_2max = $ to 4.5 liters

often you wish to compete and in which sports, each week of the training year can be planned according to available training time and facilities to effectively prepare you for meeting your goals.

Five Training Stages

Ideally, preparation for competitive endurance sports includes five stages: Base, Intensity, Peak, Competition (or Race), and Restoration. The number of weeks given each stage depends on the number of competitive seasons planned per year and your experience and condition. The physiological purposes of the five training stages will be explained in detail in chapter 3. It is necessary at this point only to understand that there are essential physiological developments that take place by stages in a progressive fashion during the weeks and months preceding competition. Figure 2.2 illustrates the five training stages for an athlete participating in one competition season per year. It is helpful in planning to consider actual dates for competitions, training camps, clinics, and any medical or physiological testing desired during the year.

Training Cycles

The 52 weeks of the year (assuming one competition season per year) are next divided into shorter training cycles. Most commonly employed are 4-week cycles, but some athletes and coaches use cycles of different lengths. Depending on the stage of the year, each of these cycles has its own "personality," which is planned to elicit the proper training response for that stage of the year.

Regardless of your experience, the number of competition seasons per year, and the total amount of time (Year Hours) for training, every training plan accounts for a total of 100% of the year's available training time. Each 4-week cycle must therefore consist of a certain percentage of this total. Table 2.2 illustrates this point. Several factors dictate the percentage of the year's total volume assigned to each 4-week cycle.

First, the stage of the year must be considered. Typically, training during the Base stage is of low intensity and low-to-moderate training volume. As the weeks progress, a greater volume of training is introduced, and the number of high-intensity workouts per week begins to increase.

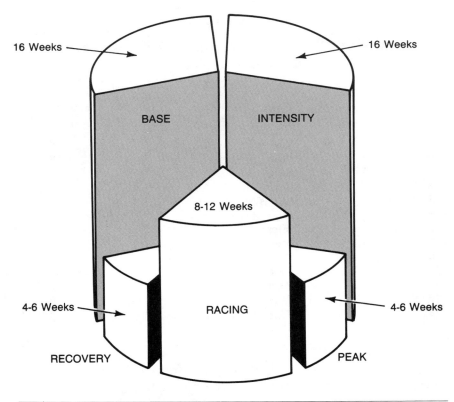

Figure 2.2 The five training stages of the year.

The Intensity stage is marked by a progressive increase in both intensity and volume. Typically, this stage has the highest volume per 4-week cycle of any stage during the year.

The Peak stage is characterized by less total training volume, but by high-intensity and "sharpening" workouts. The Competition stage typically has high intensity, yet markedly reduced volume per cycle. The Restoration stage is always characterized by very low volume and intensity, with training accomplished by alternative activities much of the time.

Caution should be exercised when determining the volume increase from one 4-week cycle to the next, especially during the Intensity stage. Too much training too soon will result in overtraining.

As mentioned earlier, each 4-week cycle will have its own personality, or format for eliciting the desired physiological training response. Planning this aspect of the cycle is critical because each cycle must prepare you for the next; some experience with successful training

---

Table 2.2

4-Week Training Cycles as Percentage of Yearly Training Volume

Cycle	Stage	% Year hours
1	Base	6
2	Base	7
3	Base	8
4	Base	9
5	Intensity	9
6	Intensity	10
7	Intensity	11
8	Intensity	9
9	Peak	8
10	Race	7
11	Race	7
12	Race	6
13	Regeneration	3
	Total	100

plans is helpful in designing each cycle's format. Basically, this involves first deciding the categories of training to be used as well as the relative intensity for each one. Though other categories may be used, the training categories used in this book include Speed Work, Endurance and Overdistance training, Race/Pace intensities, Interval and Vertical methods, and Strength training. (These are defined in chapter 4.) Next, the percentage of each of these categories used in a given cycle is determined, taking into consideration the stage of the year, your experience, your overall training base, and the sport. For example, if you are lacking in strength, then more of the total training volume must be allocated to improving strength.

Figure 2.3 illustrates a typical division of the percentages of each training component per 4-week cycle. Chapter 3 will discuss in detail the physiological rationale for planning this way. Later you'll have an opportunity to exercise your own ideas and experiences for this planning phase.

The Weekly Pattern for the 4-Week Cycle

Physiologically, the optimal training response is derived through training cycles that have weekly patterns designed around the following considerations:

Predictable Pattern

First, it is desirable that the training pattern be similar from week to week and therefore predictable. For example, Overdistance (long, slow distance) workouts might fit in best on Saturdays or Sundays. Also, the pattern of the few days just before competitions is important and must be designed appropriately. Creating the pattern depends on the logistics of work or school commitments, your individual preferences (such as time of day for workouts, days of the week when a certain facility is available, number of workouts that can be done per day, etc.), team workout schedule, and competition schedule. You may need to try several weekly patterns to find the best one. It is wise to

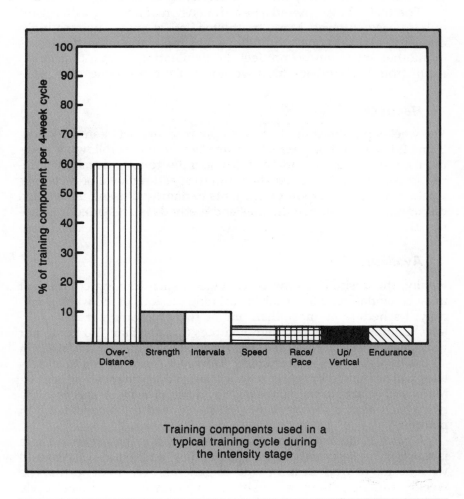

Figure 2.3 Percentage of training components in a 4-week cycle.

remain flexible about the weekly pattern so that you can make necessary changes according to other changes in schedule that might occur, such as with family, work, and school.

Intensity

The intensity of each workout is important to consider when creating the weekly pattern. Typically, a "hard" workout should be followed by an "easy" workout. The "hard day–easy day" routine has been popular with athletes and coaches for some time. However, many athletes require 2 easy days following a hard day. Again, you and your coach need to rely on past experience in deciding this issue.

Triathletes have entered a new dimension of training with regard to hard/easy patterns. Many triathletes "cross-train," using a high-intensity session in one sport followed by moderate-to-hard sessions in another sport, yet do not feel the debilitating fatigue that might result from back-to-back hard workouts using the same muscles.

Recovery

The weekly pattern should allow proper recovery between workouts. Some types of training actually promote restoration following high-intensity exercise. Low-intensity, moderate- to long-duration training serves to promote circulation and to speed removal of metabolic waste from and transport of nutrients to damaged tissue. A detailed discussion of restorative theories and methods is presented in chapter 10.

Available Time

Finally, the desired volume percentage of each training component must be worked into the available training sessions of the week. Typically, I schedule no more than one or two workouts per day. Athletes training at extremely high volumes (greater than 750 hours per year) may need to schedule three training sessions per day to fit in all the necessary types of training. However, most citizen-level athletes will be limited by work, school, family, and other commitments. Many will be able to train once per day during the week and possibly twice each day on the weekend. This will need to be considered in planning.

Figure 2.4 illustrates three different weekly training patterns. There is much room for variation here, depending on the time of year and what seems to work best for you. In general, I recommend that the weekly training pattern be consistent for each week of a 4-week cycle and fairly consistent from cycle to cycle. Of course, there will need

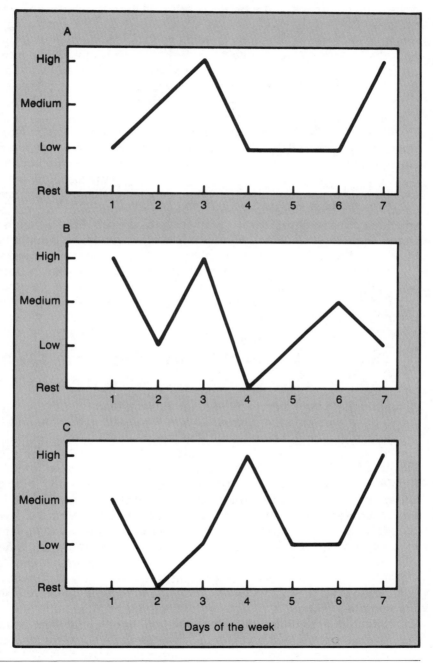

Figure 2.4 Examples of different weekly patterns and associated stress loads.

to be subtle changes in the patterns as the stages of the training year progress toward the Competition stage. However, the basic framework of the weekly pattern can remain much the same. For example, Overdistance days can remain on Sundays throughout the year, Strength days can remain on the days when facilities are available, and days that will be designated Race/Pace days during the Peak and Competition stages can be high-intensity Interval days or Pace days during the Intensity stage.

Consistent weekly patterns can promote recovery between workouts, reduce psychological stress that might otherwise be caused by constantly changing schedules, and very gradually tune the body for the Competition stage. Predetermined training patterns allow for an organized, sensible, and fluid progression of the training stimuli. Scattered, inconsistent training may be likened to the sound of the instruments of an orchestra as the players warm up—erratic, meaningless noise. The presence of the conductor leading the musicians suddenly organizes the noise of each instrument into a delightful melody.

However, remember that the ideal situation is subject to upset and that you'll need to be flexible and occasionally rework the weekly pattern to accommodate changes because of work, illness, or other factors.

The Periodization of Training Over Each 4-Week Cycle

Periodization is the structuring of the training load for a given cycle to produce a progressive increase of training stress (volume and intensity) in a staircase fashion for the first 3 weeks of the cycle, followed by steeply reduced volume during the 4th week of the cycle to allow for adequate recovery, restoration, and adaptation from the 3 buildup weeks. Figure 2.5 illustrates this staircase effect. Of course, the periodization will be somewhat different if you use training cycles of different lengths than 4 weeks. The keys in structuring the periodization are selecting the correct increase in training load from week to week and inserting low-volume rest weeks at the appropriate times.

The 4-week cycle seems to be the most common length used by top athletes and coaches. It is not uncommon for top athletes and coaches to plan the last week of each cycle to include different training activities, games, a change in training environments, or special treats such as extra massages. One ski team, after a particularly difficult 3-week training buildup, took a trip to the French Riviera for some warm sun, beaches, and easier training. Sounds good to me!

It is plausible that the 4-week cycle might have a different periodization pattern than that described above. For example, one might plan

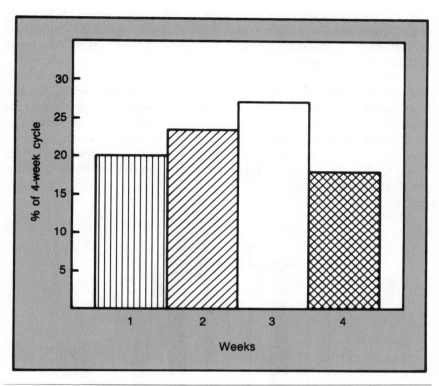

Figure 2.5 Periodization within the 4-week cycle.

the first week as a hard week with higher volume, the second week as an easy week with lower volume, the third week like the first, and the last week of the cycle like the second week. The options are many. The key is to experiment with the periodization patterns and to consider the stage of training.

Periodization can also take place from cycle to cycle. In other words, the volume of training in the first cycle of the year may be slightly less than the second cycle, and so on until the highest volume is reached during the last cycle of the Intensity stage. Figure 2.6 illustrates periodization from cycle to cycle during a year long training program.

Traditionally, many training programs have been designed without considering the need for periodization. It is not uncommon to observe athletes who train the same way, including volume and intensity, week in and week out. Other experts recommend a 5% to 10% training volume increase each week, every week. The problem with this approach is that there is no planned recovery week in which the body can adapt to the increased demands of the previous weeks. As a result, many athletes experience overtraining or injury, which ultimately forces them to take recovery time. Periodization offers the distinction of varying workloads each week, allowing for high stress one week and low stress another.

The structure of periodization within each 4-week cycle is subject to your individual experiences, proven methods used by top athletes and coaches, and the stage of the year. For example, during the Base stage, a 23, 26, 29, 22% periodization might be best. However, during the Intensity stage, a 21, 27, 33, 19% periodization might allow a more effective stress and recovery pattern. A taper cycle before a race could have a 32, 27, 23, 18% periodization, with the race planned for the 4th week of the cycle.

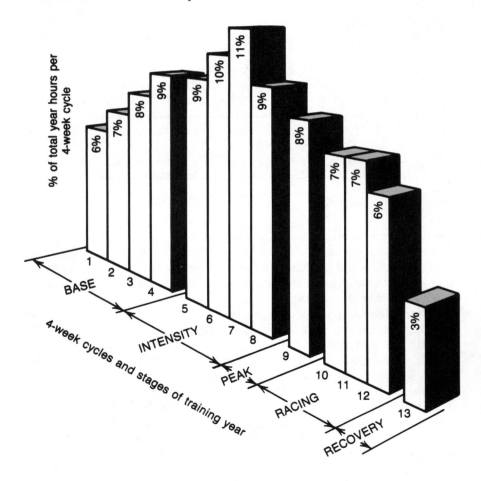

Figure 2.6 Periodization distribution between training cycles.

Training Volume in Hours per Year

The body can accommodate increases in training volume and intensity if they are applied gradually. Too much too soon, and the body will clamor for rest—or worse, may break down with injuries, fatigue, or general lethargy. Overtraining is a phenomenon usually associated with too much training before the body is prepared to adapt.

How much training is enough? That's a good question, and there are some interesting approaches to answering it. First of all, let me establish that the most common method for measuring training volume has been by measuring the distance covered and sometimes the intensity of the workouts that make up that distance. My experience with this approach has left me with reservations about it. It is difficult to determine the quality of a workout that is expressed solely in terms of distance covered. How intense in terms of percent of maximal aerobic capacity was the workout? How many minutes did it take to cover the distance? Was a predetermined time for completion of the distance adhered to, despite environmental conditions and how you were feeling? What was the physiological objective of the workout?

For example, consider a runner, training for a 10K road race, who uses a schedule in which a 6-mile run at a 6 minutes per mile pace is supposed to be a moderately easy day. If the athlete faces a stiff headwind or 90% humidity during the run and struggles to complete the workout within the time guidelines, then the entire personality of the run changes, and the physiological stress of the workout is completely different from that which was originally intended. Such factors must be taken into consideration.

The expression of training volume that I advocate and around which the information in this book is presented is *Year Hours*—the total amount of time spent training per year. After designing the structure of the training program, determining the correct volume of training in Year Hours is probably the most important decision to be made by you or your coach. Several guidelines can help you in selecting the right yearly volume.

Experience

The number of years of training in endurance sports, particularly the sport of choice, is an important consideration. An athlete with 12 years of training and competition will be able to handle a higher volume as well as a larger increase in volume from year to year if so desired. Conversely, it would be out of line for a beginner athlete to start training at high volumes.

Fitness Level

The present level of fitness will influence selection of the training volume. If you were basically inactive through the winter, it would be asking for trouble to pick up the training where it left off in the fall when you were at peak fitness after a solid racing season. Table 2.3 is designed to guide you in selecting an appropriate increase in training volume, if necessary or desired, based on past training and present level of fitness. Take a moment to estimate your present level of fitness. One way to do this is to subjectively estimate your fitness level based on your past experience. Rate yourself on a scale of 1 to 10, with 1 being totally unfit and 10 being your best fitness level ever. Then, using Table 2.3, cross-reference your training Year Hours last year and your present level of fitness to find by what percentage you should increase Year Hours for this year. Add this increase to last year's hours to obtain the new Year Hours.

Table 2.3

Recommended Percent Increase in Year Hours This Year

Year hours last year	Present level of fitness									
	1	2	3	4	5	6	7	8	9	10
<200	3	3	3	4	4	5	6	7	7	8
210-300	3	3	4	4	5	5	6	7	7	8
301-400	-	4	4	4	5	6	7	8	9	10
401-500	-	-	-	-	7	8	9	10	11	12
501-600	-	-	-	-	-	10	11	12	13	14
601-700	-	-	-	-	-	12	13	14	15	15
701-800	-	-	-	-	-	-	10	10	10	10
801-900	-	-	-	-	-	-	-	5	5	5
900-1000	-	-	-	-	-	-	-	-	-	-
>1000	-	-	-	-	-	-	-	-	-	-

Note. 1 = poor fitness level; 10 = best fitness level.

If, for example, you spent 300 hours conditioning last year (including all types of training exercises and sports) and you rate your present level of fitness a 7, then this year you would increase your Year Hours by 6% (this number is not calculated by you but is found in Table 2.3) to obtain the new figure: 318 Year Hours.

Another way of looking at this potential increase in Year Hours is to consider as a general guideline an increase of 10% to 25% per year. This works well for experienced athletes who have not trained much recently but know it is possible for their bodies to safely handle such increases. However, I do not recommend that anyone training over 400 hours per year increase volume by more than 15% per year.

Time Limitations

A third factor in determining Year Hours, especially if you are bound to a fixed amount of available training time per week, is to multiply your available weekly training time by 52 weeks to calculate a Year Hours figure. Because you have to abide by time guidelines, there will be no need to increase training time. This method works well only if your available training time does not exceed the amount you trained the last year by more than 10%.

Other commitments, such as school or work, family, social, or civic activities, will play a role when you select the training load. It's a good idea to determine a list of priorities for these commitments and see where training fits in. For example, one would be unrealistic to list training above work and family if in reality these other commitments will demand some of the time planned, but not really available, for training.

Elite Athlete Training Volumes

Another consideration in determining the correct volume of training is the standard volume used by elite athletes in the sport of choice. If top 10K runners are training only 500 hours per year, then it would probably be inappropriate and counterproductive for an inexperienced athlete to train more than that (unless training was the primary objective and competition was secondary). In chapter 6, training volumes for various levels of commitment and experience in each endurance sport are presented so that you can set an appropriate ceiling on Year Hours to train. In endurance sports, athletes who have trained for 10 years or more and who have developed the necessary physiological adaptations may be able to train fewer Year Hours with a slightly higher percentage of high-intensity work. This might not work for every experienced athlete, however; each will have to determine this individually.

If you are a coach, the information presented here can form the basis of any training plan you might wish to design. One advantage of planning this way is that each of the variables, such as workout objective, percentage of Year Hours per workout, weekly patterns, periodization within a cycle, and total Year Hours, can be changed at any time for different athletes or training goals, and you can see clearly how the changes affect the overall program. For example, if an athlete starts a training program at 550 hours per year and after 2 months decides that family commitments make this goal unrealistic, the Year Hours can be reduced without undermining the integrity of the total program.

Appropriate Activity for Each Workout

The next steps for completing the training plan involve the selection of the appropriate activity and the right intensity level for each training session planned. There are several variables to consider when assigning these. How you accomplish a given workout is subject to factors such as

1. your training philosophy,
2. past experiences,
3. training facilities that are available,
4. injuries or handicaps,
5. your present psychological state,
6. recovery from previous workouts, and
7. the specificity and technical requirements for the workout.

Training systematically allows you the opportunity to be creative within a framework. This accommodates your personal philosophy and ideas about the overall and specific aspects of the plan. If you have had good results using a certain strength routine, then this will play an important role in determining what strength workouts to schedule on the plan. Conversely, you might not have easy access to optimal strength-training equipment and, therefore, may need to improvise with a circuit routine at home.

Injuries and handicaps will dictate the type of activity to be used for a given training session. A runner with a strained hamstring muscle will be well advised to train in the water, using a flotation vest designed for water running.

A variety of activities can help prevent boredom and psychological burnout if used at the proper times during training. For example, after a particularly difficult week of training, schedule an aerobics class, a game of water polo, or a scenic hike. Training should be fun and full of variation.

Another consideration in planning each workout is recovery from previous training sessions. Occasionally it may be necessary to plan a non-sport-specific type of activity between two hard sport-specific sessions in order to encourage full recovery.

Finally, the need for specificity of training for a sport must be reflected by the workouts. A cross-country skier may need to train with roller skis for some workouts and run for others. It is best to designate a specific activity or type of movement for each workout; digressions from the original plan should be recorded for future reference and study. There are many ways to accomplish a training objective, and therein lies the opportunity to be creative and to use new information.

Intensity

The most important point to understand regarding the assignment of intensity levels is that each workout has a specific physiological objective that is dependent upon intensity. For example, Overdistance (OD) workouts must be accomplished at an intensity between 55% and 65% of maximal aerobic capacity ($\dot{V}O_2$max). The intensity level of the OD session can be monitored by checking heart rate or perceived exertion. It is important to understand the significance of intensity for each workout and to abide by the rules of each intensity level. (Intensity is discussed in greater detail in chapters 4 and 5.)

A Strong Foundation

It is necessary to view the training year in terms of objectives such as performance, physical preparation, technical preparation, tactics, psychological preparation, and any tests or standards. A systematic approach to planning the training year allows you to use sound principles of physiology in conjunction with previous experience to plot a course that will lead to peak fitness and improved performances. The steps outlined in this chapter will serve as the fundamental structure for any systematic training plan you might wish to create. Systematic training also establishes a format or template by which the results from a given training plan may be measured and adjusted effectively. The chapters that follow will help you fill in the gaps by presenting information regarding basic physiological principles and ways to monitor the training plans you have created. Chapter 6 is written with a workbook approach so that you can design your own training plans using these guidelines.

PHYSIOLOGICAL GUIDELINES FOR SYSTEMATIC TRAINING

Systematic training is most effective if certain physiological principles are followed. In chapter 2 the basic structure of a systematic training plan was outlined. The present chapter will help you understand the relationships of several key factors used when considering the overall plan.

Training Stages of the Year

I have chosen to break systematic training plans into five stages for each competitive season. The concept of using five training stages applies ideally if you are planning for one or two competitive seasons per year. However, if you are planning a shorter training season leading up to a competition phase, you should also adapt the concept of using five stages and apply this to your plans.

The five stages are referred to as Base, Intensity, Peak, Racing, and Restoration. Each stage represents distinct physiological, neuromuscular, and psychological developmental phases necessary for systematically developing your conditioning. The graph in Figure 3.1 illustrates the characteristics of each stage in terms of percentages of

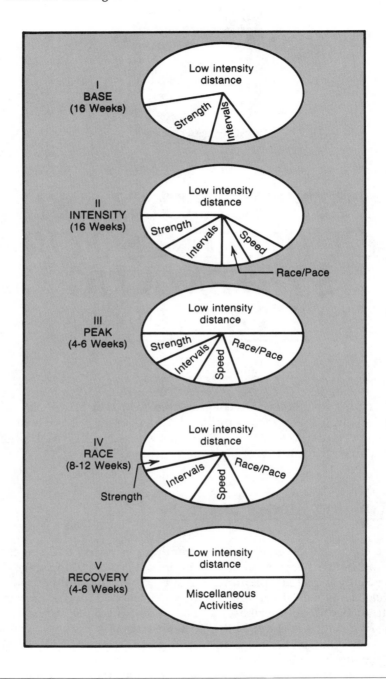

Figure 3.1 Training components emphasized during the five training stages of the year.

each training component. Ideally, there will be a subtle distinction between successive stages as training volume and emphasis change appropriately from one training cycle to the next.

The following is an overview of the five stages of training. Understanding them will help you decide upon the necessary training components for each stage of your plan. Additionally, you can use the terminology presented to build your training vocabulary.

Stage I: Base (Aerobic Buildup Phase)

The Base stage should be 20 weeks in length if you plan for 1 racing season per year, 8 to 10 weeks for a plan including 2 racing seasons per year, and as short as 4 weeks if you plan a shorter training program or several short programs per year. The predominant features of the Base stage are aerobic buildup, with a high percentage of Overdistance and Endurance work; and Strength, both nonspecific and sport-specific. Race/Pace, Intervals, and Speed work will be used little or not at all during the first 75% of this stage. Gradually, during the later weeks, a greater percentage of these components is included.

Aerobic Buildup

The primary reasons for establishing a sound aerobic base during this stage are related to energy and oxygen transport mechanisms. It is recommended that a high percentage (60-70%) of the total training volume during the Base stage be devoted to Overdistance and Endurance/Easy Distance training, which will be described in detail in chapter 4. Koivisto, Hendler, and Nadel (1982) demonstrated that improvements in fat oxidation occur with regular training at intensities of 55% to 60% of $\dot{V}O_2$max. Training at this intensity and duration also improves the muscles' blood capillary density and mitochondria numbers and efficiency, all of which contribute to improved oxygen transport and energy use at the cellular level. These adaptations will be described in detail in chapter 4.

Strength

The Base stage provides the opportunity to emphasize Strength training for improving overall strength as well as sport-specific strength. Approximately 10% to 20% of total training time during this stage should be Strength work, depending on your abilities.

Most endurance sports require moderate strength. A basic requirement of all endurance sports is the ability of the muscles to contract repeatedly with force and quickness throughout a race. More difficult to determine, however, is the amount and type of Strength training to be employed in the overall plan.

The primary goal for Strength training during the Base stage is to place the muscles under sufficient loads so that they adapt or accommodate to the loads. When adaptation has occurred, the loads may be increased. Typically, muscles improve in strength when placed under loads of greater than two thirds of maximum strength.

There are many methods for increasing strength. Weight machines, free weights, calisthenics, plyometrics, and rubber tubing devices all work well. In general, most Strength exercises should simulate the motions used in competition, thereby strengthening sport-specific muscles and connective tissue. However, during the Base stage, it is less critical to be completely sport-specific in Strength exercises. The physiological details of Strength training are discussed more in chapter 4. Actual Strength workouts and recommendations for each sport are outlined in Appendix A. Refer to these for specific guidance in doing sport-specific Strength routines.

Stage II: Intensity

The intensity stage should be 16 weeks in length if you plan for one racing season per year, 4 to 8 weeks for a plan including two racing seasons per year, and as short as 4 weeks if you plan a shorter program.

This stage brings an increase in overall training stress in terms of greater volume (hours) and intensity with specific Speed, Interval, Race/Pace, and Vertical Intervals. It is recommended that a high percentage of this stage's total training volume (50-60%) be planned as low-intensity aerobic training through Overdistance and Endurance/Easy Distance activities in order to maintain the aerobic base established earlier. However, more time is devoted to higher intensity training than in the Base stage. Intervals, Race/Pace, and Speed workouts will improve the body's ability to sustain high-intensity effort for longer periods of time, which is the requirement of competition. The amount of these higher intensity components must be increased gradually throughout this stage so the body can adapt adequately. These training components will be discussed in greater detail in chapter 4.

Easy Speed work teaches the body to learn pace and, very gradually, coordinated movement at faster-than-race pace. Intervals on flat and hilly terrain allow you to develop a subjective sense of "threshold" (described in detail in chapter 5) and to train at high intensity yet maintain control and not exceed the threshold. As the stage progresses, designated Pace workouts and early season Races will be introduced to the program. These will provide benchmarks for measuring progress and for working out any technical and psychological bugs well before the competitive season arrives.

The important factor in Race/Pace workouts during the Intensity stage is that the efforts are not all out. Rather, you should attempt to accomplish these workouts at your present level of fitness, staying under control in terms of the psychological and emotional investment in the workout. Too much high-intensity racing early in the season may lead to premature peaking or burnout. Approaching a Race or Pace workout during this stage with a specific purpose, such as trying a new strategy for en route intake of energy drinks or testing a new pair of skis or a specific warm-up routine, will enhance the learning and preparation for the upcoming competition season.

Stage III: Peak (Taper)

Many coaches and athletes refer to peaking as *tapering* or *sharpening*; the terms are synonymous. This stage (usually 4 to 8 weeks in length) is characterized by a decrease in training volume from the Intensity stage. However, the intensity of certain training components, such as Speed, Intervals, and one or two Race/Pace workouts, will typically be very high in order to refine technique and energy systems at high speeds. Simultaneously, about 50% of the training volume will be low-intensity aerobic training through Overdistance and Endurance/Easy Distance activities in order to maintain the aerobic base. The Peak stage is also characterized by an emphasis on restoration and recovery from training so that the body may become fully rested and energy stores completely replenished prior to intense competition. Restoration will be discussed in detail in chapter 10.

Stage IV: Racing

Ideally, the plan will have been successfully carried out and you will be at optimal racing capabilities at this stage. Depending on you and the design of your training plan, peak racing form and top racing will last 8 to 16 weeks. Some sports, such as cycling, may involve slightly longer Racing seasons, and this must be reflected in the overall plan. Approximately 50% of total training time during this stage will be Overdistance in order to maintain the aerobic base and provide active recovery training. Interval training will comprise another 10% to 15% of total training, Speed work will be about 10% of total, and Racing will constitute the remaining time. The races will be very demanding physiologically. That, coupled with the stresses of travel, change of diet, and psychological adjustment, will wear you down. It is essential that you employ an active restoration/recovery routine during this stage. (See chapter 10 for specific guidelines on proper recovery methods.)

Stage V: Restoration

After a competitive period, it is recommended that about 4 to 8 weeks be devoted to active recovery. This stage is characterized by a reduced training volume and low-intensity training. An emphasis is placed on using alternative training methods in a variety of terrain. It is also beneficial to incorporate some team sports such as soccer or volleyball once in a while to break up the routine. If you are coaching, this approach works especially well for younger athletes. The key to all training in this stage is that it be less structured and have variety.

Specificity of Training

Each sport places different physiological, biomechanical, and psychological demands on the body. Endurance sports such as running, the triathlon, cycling, swimming, aerobics, hiking, and cross-country skiing require efficient aerobic metabolism, strength, anaerobic metabolism, and neuromuscular coordination for efficient technique. Each sport has a different technical or biomechanical requirement that must be met for you to develop efficient movements.

When deciding which sport activity to use for training workouts, you must consider several factors simultaneously: technique, conditioning, recovery, injury prevention, and psychological freshness. The type of training you use should relate closely to the specific action that will be used in competition. In this way the time, tempo, speed, and intensity of the training activity will lead to sport-specific results in the metabolic pathways and energy systems used, the muscle fiber types recruited, and the various organs and systems used during that exercise. For example, if you want to become a top triathlete but never practice swimming at race pace, your stroke mechanics and swim conditioning will remain subpar.

However, a balance must be maintained between sport-specific conditioning and technique work on the one hand and proper recovery, injury prevention, and psychological freshness on the other. For

example, a runner who trains by running on pavement for every workout may be subject to an increased likelihood of injury and psychological staleness. If that same runner rode a bicycle, went cross-country
skiing, or did some water running in the deep end of the pool once
in a while, aerobic conditioning probably would not suffer, yet the
running-specific muscles and connective tissue would get a break, and
the athlete might gain a refreshing perspective on the overall training plan. Cross-training, which is the use of a variety of aerobic
activities for training, has become very popular among endurance athletes. Triathletes have discovered the benefits of triple-sport fitness,
and many claim that the variety of activities balances training stress
and enhances their motivation. Cross-country skiers have long used
a variety of activities to cross-train during the dryland season (Figure
3.2). Many top runners use cycling, water running, swimming, and
cross-country skiing during the Base period to allow full recovery of
the running muscles, enhance endurance and strength, and avoid psychological burnout.

Figure 3.2 Roller skiing is the next best thing to being on snow
for sport-specific training.

These factors considered, it is still essential that a certain percentage of the training be completely specific to the requirements of competition in the chosen sport. In general, it is best to train more specifically as the competitive season approaches—usually focusing on sport specificity in the middle of the Intensity stage. Aerobic conditioning in the sport-specific muscles will become sharpened. Perhaps more importantly, the neuromuscular coordination for sport-specific technique will be refined. In all endurance sports, particularly cycling, cross-country skiing, and swimming, efficient technique and form are critical for improvements in competition. For the cross-country skier, the best training will be to ski, ski, ski. The cyclist must ride, ride, ride, particularly with a group to learn and refine the technical aspects of riding in a pack. The swimmer or triathlete must practice stroke mechanics to improve efficiency. The key is to cross-train wisely, keeping the sport-specific goals in mind and practicing the sport as much as is appropriate, given the variables described above.

Adaptation

Stressing the body in training will bring subtle changes as the body adapts to these imposed demands. Improved circulation, respiratory function, heart function, increased muscle endurance, strength, and power, and sturdier connective tissue, tendons, ligaments, and bones are all part of the body's adaptation to appropriate training stress. Athletes who train too much or too fast too soon are likely candidates for illness or injury, having overstressed the body so it could not adapt.

Overload

The body will improve if an appropriate load imposes a demand on the body's systems. As the body adapts to training, an increased workload stimulates further improvements in conditioning. This relates to the gradual increases in time and intensity throughout the Base and Intensity stages, which are intended to impose enough demand on the body to stimulate growth. Endurance overload will allow the energy systems and the oxygen transport systems to adapt. The contractile proteins in muscles will increase if there is a strength overload.

Progression and Periodization

The body will adapt well to an imposed training overload if there is a proper progression. If training loads are increased too much too soon, the body cannot adapt and grow stronger—rather, it will weaken and break down. Several factors must be considered in formulating the correct progression. The weekly pattern and the number of sessions per week, the percentage of the total year's training volume used in a particular cycle, the stage of the competitive season, the percentage of low- versus high-intensity training, and the periodization pattern for a given training cycle—all will influence the body's ability to adapt.

The progression from week to week and cycle to cycle need not be a steady increase in training time and intensity. A periodization pattern for a given training cycle should allow a staircase progression that overloads the body for the first 3 weeks, followed by a week of decreased training volume and intensity (see Figure 3.3). Also, a

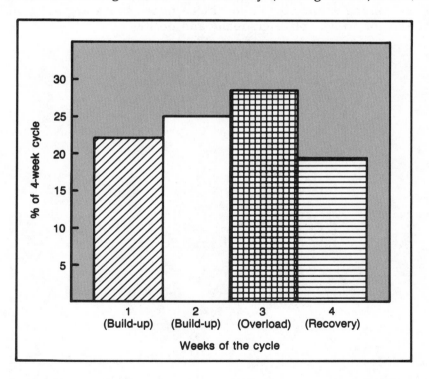

Figure 3.3 Periodization of build–up, overload, and recovery in a 4-week training cycle.

progression in training volume and intensity should take place from cycle to cycle, thereby gradually overloading the system. Using progression in training means taking a bit more time to gradually build up conditioning, but it makes it far easier for the body to adapt to than does an overly aggressive approach.

Those athletes with limited or constant training time available may need to modify the periodization patterns within a training cycle. For example, if you have a ceiling on the amount of time to train each week, simply train slightly less than this amount every other week or on the last week of the cycle to promote adequate recovery.

Long-term training progressions from year to year will lead to substantial improvements. Most of the best endurance athletes reach their highest performance potentials only after many years of training and competition. Gradual physiological development, refinement of technical skills, education about strategy, and personal development and maturation all lead to steady improvements over the years. Today's top endurance athletes did not start training at 700 hours per year. Instead, they started as young athletes and progressively increased their training volume by 5% to 10% each year to allow growth and adaptation to take place gradually and positively.

SERIOUS *TRAINING:*
A MODEL
SYSTEMATIC
TRAINING
PROGRAM

A s mentioned in chapter 1, training can be considered a language unto itself, with many different words, phrases, and definitions. When it comes to endurance sports training, we speak a variety of dialects. *Intervals* may mean something completely different to one person than to another.

The systematic approach to planning and implementing training programs serves as a universal translator, even though people may continue to speak slightly different dialects of the training language (Figure 4.1). This is because every scheduled workout is assigned a specific time and intensity. These two components, combined with knowledge of the activity or sport used in the training session, will elicit a specific physiological response from the workout. Standardizing workouts by indicating time and intensity also allows you or your coach to measure the relative value of the particular method of training or technique pattern used. Adjustments in the training plan can be made expeditiously and on an informed basis either during a particular training stage or season or at the beginning of a new planning phase.

Though systematic training in itself serves as an effective translator, we can clarify the language even further if we define the actual

Figure 4.1 Training partners often discuss training methods but sometimes seem to be speaking different languages. The SERIOUS system can provide the missing link.

training components and the reasons for incorporating them into training plans at various stages of the year. With this in mind, I have created an acronym to serve as a teaching tool to enhance learning and promote standardization of the language of training. SERIOUS is the acronym, with the components delineated as follows:

S = SPEED
E = ENDURANCE or EASY DISTANCE
R = RACE or PACE
I = INTERVAL
O = OVERDISTANCE
U = UP or VERTICAL INTERVAL
S = STRENGTH

These seven training components, each defined in terms of relative time, intensity, and technical purpose, can be used to compose any conceivable training plan for an endurance athlete. Incorporating them into a systematic plan greatly reduces language barriers and expedites learning. For example, if two athletes are training systematically and use clearly defined SERIOUS components as part of their plan, they can effectively communicate with each other regarding various ways to accomplish a given objective. Knowing the duration and intensity of any workout allows you to clearly understand its purpose and enhances the outcome of each training session.

Each of the seven SERIOUS components has been referred to in many ways by various coaches, physiologists, and athletes over the years. The remainder of this chapter is devoted to defining each SERIOUS component in terms of its physiological purpose and in terms of its time and intensity. An attempt is made at describing the various synonyms that have been used by others. Included with these definitions are descriptions of how to actually accomplish each type of workout and to apply these concepts to your chosen sport. Sport-specific instructions for each SERIOUS component are provided in Appendix C.

Speed

Speed is what racing is all about. We need to teach the muscles to move fast (Figure 4.2). Sharkey (1984) defines speed as the combination of reaction time (time from stimulus to the start of movement) and movement time (time to complete the movement). Requirements for speed vary depending upon the activity.

Another variable for speed rests with your muscle fiber types. Each of us is born with a certain number of muscle fibers that are either "fast twitch" or "slow twitch" in nature. Fast-twitch (FT) muscle fibers have the ability to contract, or fire, rapidly upon stimulation. These fibers allow the body to generate speed. However, fast-twitch muscle fibers exhaust rather quickly when used at maximum effort, usually tiring within the first 2 minutes of speed-burst activity, depleting their energy stores within this time. However, it takes only a few minutes of recovery to replenish those energy stores.

Slow-twitch (ST) muscle fibers have the ability to contract at a moderate speed over a prolonged period of time. At a moderate intensity of exercise, these fibers might contract over and over again for hours before fatiguing. They rely on the aerobic energy system for supplying fuel for contraction. Oxygen enters the blood, is carried to the muscle cells, mixes with glycogen (and free fatty acids)

Figure 4.2 Speed work should be part of your total plan.

within the cell in a process called *oxidation*, and energy is released so the muscle fiber can contract. The cycle can continue over a long time, given enough fuel and oxygen. This is the system primarily used for all endurance activities.

It is important to understand that your body is composed of a certain percentage of fast- and slow-twitch muscle fibers. The percentage of each is genetically determined and cannot be changed. Most people have a fairly well-balanced combination of close to 50% fast- and 50% slow-twitch fibers. World-class endurance athletes generally have a greater percentage of slow-twitch fibers. For example, Costill (1979) conducted muscle biopsy tests revealing that among elite U.S. distance runners, 90% of gastrocnemius (calf) muscle is composed of ST fibers, whereas elite sprinters may have 90% FT fibers.

It is interesting to test yourself to get an idea of your muscle fiber composition. Some indicators include these:

- Vertical jump: If you can jump 16 inches or more from a standing start, you probably have more FT than ST in your thigh and calf muscles.
- If you were always the fastest runner on the block for short distances but couldn't keep up over longer distances, you may be a fast twitcher.

- If you can run, bike, swim, or hike all day at a moderate intensity without tiring, you're probably more of a slow twitcher.

Regardless of your fiber type composition, you can train fast-twitch fibers to move faster, to have more available energy, and to recover more quickly after exhaustive exercise. Most importantly, you can teach your muscle fibers to move faster. The neuromuscular pathways used for coordinating fast movement will be improved, facilitating smooth, relaxed, and coordinated movement. Whether it be for passing a competitor or avoiding a determined dog, you need to incorporate speed into your plan.

Many coaches and athletes use the word *speed* as a catchall for several different types of training. Speed has been used to describe short (15- to 30-second), intense repeats; long and short, intense intervals; racing and pace workouts; easy and relaxed 200-meter speed intervals; and easy 5-second pickups (acceleration periods) used during distance training.

In the SERIOUS system, Speed work is considered a low-intensity effort, and the amount of time per session is small, as is Speed's percentage of the total training volume. The amount of Speed work in a given cycle will depend on the stage of the year and the number of hours you are training that year. Typically, formal Speed work begins in the early weeks of the Intensity stage and continues through the Racing stage. However, it is important to incorporate a small amount of Speed in the Base stage as well. I refer to the Speed training during the Base stage as tempo speed bursts. Basically, they are short, 5- to 8-second pickups of speed initiated every 15 to 20 minutes during long, slow, distance-training sessions. The intensity is low, yet the movement should be at a quick tempo and relaxed. Tempo speed bursts are ideally used throughout the year.

Formal Speed work (Body Speeds in the SERIOUS system) must always be accompanied by a certain state of mind. Many images persist in our minds, reinforced by our sports magazines, of the sprinter breaking the finish tape with clenched fists and tense face. These images imply incredibly hard work. However, Speed work for endurance sports must be accomplished with as little tension as possible. It must be referred to as *easy speed*. The endurance athlete must search the body for a reserve of speed and "release" it, much like the archer releases the arrow from the bow. The neuromuscular mechanisms are then in place, ready to receive and remember the feelings of that release of speed.

An analogy describes the need for Speed training as an integral part of endurance sports training plans. We all have neuromuscular pathways leading from the brain to the muscles. These pathways can be likened to a path across a meadow. If the path is walked on frequently, the grass cannot grow over the path, and the way remains clear. However, if we discontinue using the path, the grass will grow over, and it will become difficult to find the way. Thus, it is important to use Speed training throughout the year to develop and maintain clear neuromuscular pathways from the brain to the muscles employed in the specific activity.

Typically, Body Speed sessions consist of 20 to 45 minutes of repeated speed bursts, each lasting between 30 and 60 seconds at low intensity, with about 1 or 2 minutes of recovery between sprints. The key to Speed work is the ability to perform it without tension. Let your bones move you while your muscles hang on for the ride. Do not force the speed, but let it release very gradually; improve your speed only a little every week or two. It requires a bit of concentration and discipline at first, but soon you'll feel the essence of easy speed.

Endurance or Easy Distance

Endurance is defined as the ability to withstand stress over prolonged periods—in the case of endurance sports, prolonged physical stress. All training plans must include a certain amount of endurance work. In the SERIOUS system, Endurance/Easy Distance and Overdistance training are important components for developing and maintaining aerobic endurance. These training components are accomplished at low intensity (see chapter 5) and for considerable lengths of time (between 30 and 60 minutes for Endurance/Easy Distance and between 60 and 180 minutes or more for Overdistance). A high percentage of the total training volume is devoted to Endurance and Overdistance training—between 50% and 80% (combined), depending on the stage of the year: during the Base stage, about 80%, gradually falling to about 50% during Racing. Specifically, Endurance/Easy Distance training sessions are used as warm-up and cool-down for more intense exercise, such as Interval, Race/Pace, Up/Vertical Interval, and Strength. Also, this component may be planned as a workout in itself, usually lasting no longer than 60 minutes and being performed at low intensity (Figure 4.3).

The endurance workouts outlined for your sport are primarily dedicated to improving aerobic capacity. *Aerobic* describes exercise that takes place in the presence of oxygen supplied to the muscle tissues via the cardiorespiratory system. This type of exercise is at minimum 10 continuous minutes in duration. The other type of exercise is called *anaerobic*, meaning without oxygen. Anaerobic exercise occurs whenever the oxygen demands exceed the oxygen supplies of the cardiorespiratory system. Usually anaerobic exercise consists of short-burst, high-intensity effort, which produces lactic acid, a metabolic byproduct. Lactic acid is the substance that, if accumulated in significant quantity in the system, may cause fatigue, labored breathing, discomfort, and a sense of distress.

Endurance training accomplishes many things. It increases your body's ability to consume oxygen ($\dot{V}O_2$max), increases the size and number of the mitochondria in muscle cells (mitochondria are little powerhouses within each muscle cell), increases the size and number of blood capillaries, and improves aerobic enzymes for carbohydrate and fat metabolism. These changes are described in greater detail in the discussion on Overdistance training and in chapter 5 on Intensity. In short, endurance exercise improves your body's ability to deliver the goods to your muscles so that they adapt, grow stronger, and become better at prolonged effort.

Figure 4.3 Endurance/Easy Distance training time is a great opportunity to try cross-training with alternative activities, such as rowing with the Concept II rowing ergometer.

Race/Pace

Races are opportunities to test the results of systematic training. Competitions, regardless of size, form, place, or time, are ways you can learn to feel good about yourself. They are the culmination of the training process, and they are the goals to strive for—and in the striving, you learn many things about yourself and your capabilities (Figure 4.4).

Figure 4.4 Races test the effectiveness of your plan. However, it's important to keep a good smile on your face!

During the Base, Intensity, and Peak stages prior to the racing season, some Race/Pace workouts should be scheduled. These workouts are intended to be used as benchmarks for determining the effectiveness and progress of the training plan. Pace workouts, timed trials, and organized race events will all serve this purpose. They will also maintain motivation for training prior to the racing season and help you work out the ''bugs'' in technique, equipment, and strategy.

The essential point of these early Race/Pace workouts is to help you measure the pace you are going at that date, given your current fitness level. It is very important that you recognize the difference between maximum effort and the effort possible at your current fitness level. *Maximum effort* means an all-out effort, which will be used during the racing season. *Current fitness level* assumes that you are still building your conditioning and that your body is not quite ready to be pushed to on all-out effort.

These workouts should be done at the prescribed intensity and time outlined in the yearly plan. All Race/Pace workouts, particularly in the stages preceeding the Competition stage, should be approached with an attitude of control, low stress, and search for knowledge; your concentrating on moving smoothly; and with regard to your body's inner language. A great deal may be learned from these trials. These are great times to test yourself on a variety of factors, including technique, equipment changes, strategies, feed schedules, prerace diets, concentration, and, of course, your conditioning.

For the latter, one way to test your level of fitness is to use the same measured course (approximately half the distance you will be racing in season—this depends on the length of the planned races and the stage of the season) every 3rd or 4th week. Perform the course at a predetermined intensity (heart rate monitors work well for this purpose), measuring your time to check for improvement. The other weeks, use a different course and, while paying some attention to time and distance, focus more on your subjective feelings. The amount of time for these timed trials will vary depending on the stage of training you are in.

The keys to becoming a better racer are efficient movement, control and self-discipline, and the knowledge you gain by listening to your body. The most accomplished endurance athletes have been competing for many years. The lessons they have learned have come by many hours of practice, trial and error, and a systematic approach to analyzing performance through self-reflection.

Intervals

The training jargon describing intervals is variable and inconsistent. In the SERIOUS system, Intervals are repeated work efforts ranging from 1 to 10 minutes and of high intensity (see chapter 5 for intensity guidelines). Intervals can be used on a variety of terrains, but in the SERIOUS system, I prefer to distinguish these from Up/Vertical Intervals by specifying that they be completed on flat, slightly downhill, or rolling terrain.

Up/Vertical Intervals are specifically used on moderate to steep hills in order to recruit the muscle fibers used in climbing. However, the intensity effort is the same for Intervals and Up/Vertical Intervals.

Interval training challenges your body's ability to carry and deliver oxygen to the muscle cells for short periods of fairly intense work before too much lactic acid builds up. Remember those fast-twitch muscle fibers we discussed earlier? There are two types of fast-twitch fibers—fast glycolytic (FG) and fast oxidative glycolytic (FOG). FG fibers do not have the ability to use oxygen in the fueling process. They use only the fuel stored in their cells. Once that fuel is spent, the fibers fatigue until a period of recovery allows the fuel to be replenished.

On the other hand, FOG fibers do have the potential to use oxygen if trained appropriately. FOG fibers contract somewhat more rapidly and fatigue faster than slow-twitch fibers do. Interval training recruits the FOG fibers to perform the faster, more intense efforts experienced in a 2-to-10 minute bout of exercise. Training at the appropriate intensity stimulates the FOG muscles to adapt and improve their aerobic capacity. The bottom line for Interval training is that as your FOG fibers improve their oxidative capabilities, so should your ability to work at a higher percentage of maximum oxygen uptake capacity improve.

Let's look at an example. Say you train at the same intensity, speed, and duration all the time, such as 30 minutes of Endurance/Easy Distance 5 times per week. If you try picking up the pace significantly, you will likely find that you fatigue rapidly. This is because those FOG fibers you are recruiting to make you go faster are not trained to handle the newly imposed demands. Their oxidative energy supplies are limited, and an accumulation of lactic acid occurs, resulting in a variety of subjective feelings that tell you you won't be able to keep up the pace for long. Physiologists call this the anaerobic threshold (AT) or onset of blood lactate accumulation(OBLA). You can improve your AT and thus improve performance. How?

Intervals. Training with intervals can raise your AT significantly if you do not regularly push the intensity over 75% of maximum effort. Top endurance athletes maintain an AT of 80% to 90% of $\dot{V}O_2max$, as contrasted with unfit individuals who maintain an AT around 50% of $\dot{V}O_2max$. I've worked with elite cross-country skiers who have recorded ATs of 95% $\dot{V}O_2max$. This means that in races they can ski at near-maximum intensity before fatigue from lactic acid accumulation limits their performance.

It makes good sense to include a healthy dose of Interval training in your weekly plan. How much you include depends upon the stage of the training year and your yearly training volume. Typically, Intervals make up about 5% of training time in the Base stage and 10% to 15% of total training volume during the Intensity, Peak, and Racing stages. The proper intensity to use for Interval training is described in detail in chapter 5.

Intervals take several forms (Figure 4.5). There are long intervals and short intervals, Fartlek and natural intervals, track intervals and pace intervals. Each type of interval has pretty much the same function—to place a demand on your muscles so that the FOG fibers are recruited and their oxidative capabilities improved. The bottom line is that you'll be able to go farther and faster with less fatigue.

Figure 4.5 Intervals can be done on a measured course or Fartlek style. Here, elite runner Jim Miller demonstrates good form during 400-meter repeats.

Overdistance

Here lies the heart of the SERIOUS system for endurance sports. In every stage of the year, the greatest percentage of the total training volume is reserved for Overdistance (OD) training.

Overdistance does not mean overdoing it. Think of Overdistance as the way to a basic aerobic foundation—long, easy hikes in the mountains; leisurely bicycle rides in the country, rarely shifting to your large front sprocket; the weekly long, slow, distance run; a 2-hour-long ski, concentrating on technique. These exemplify Overdistance (Figure 4.6).

Figure 4.6 NCAA cross-country ski champion Brenda White and Rossi out for the long run. Overdistance workouts are intended to feel "guilt-producingly easy."

The difference between Endurance/Easy Distance and OD is the amount of time you spend on the workout. Typically, Endurance workouts are not much longer than 60 minutes. Minimum time for most OD workouts is 1 hour, and usually they exceed 1½ hours, depending on the stage of the year and the volume of training. It's a good idea to gradually build up to doing at least one OD workout per month that takes between 2 and 5 hours, in order to build up conditioning, confidence, and mental toughness. The intensity is very low, as described in chapter 5. Any harder than this, and you are not doing an OD workout. It is very common for endurance athletes to train at intensities that average about 70% to 75% of maximum ($\dot{V}O_2$) for the bulk of their training. The problems with this approach are several. First, races usually are not performed at this low an intensity. Second, training at this intensity depletes muscle glycogen faster than at lower intensity, such as OD training intensity (55% to 65% $\dot{V}O_2$max). Third, a higher production of lactic acid occurs at this intensity than at OD intensity.

The secret of OD is in the physiological changes it causes. Basically, there are two adaptations the body makes in response to OD training. First, you'll be training your body to increase its efficiency for releasing and burning free fatty acids over long distances, as enzymatic and hormonal changes in the muscle cells make it easier for fat to be utilized as fuel during long-duration exercise. This will prove valuable for long events. Also, you'll improve the body's circulatory characteristics in the peripheral muscles—those that do the work in races to help move waste products away from muscle tissue and bring new blood, oxygen, and fuel to the muscle for more work. The mitochondria, the powerhouses of the muscle cells, will increase in number and efficiency.

These physiological changes establish a foundation on which all other aspects of the SERIOUS program rely. A solid aerobic base will facilitate the delivery of oxygen and fuel to the muscles and the removal of harmful, fatiguing metabolic waste products from the muscle cells. The body will be able to function at high intensities for longer periods before the debilitating effects of high-intensity racing cause fatigue and slow you down.

The key to Overdistance training is that you make it fun and particularly easy. It's difficult sometimes to learn the true meaning of *easy*. Many athletes have the tendency to train at medium to high intensity all of the time, never allowing their bodies to rest and catch up from the rigorous training they do on other days. Self-discipline will be called upon when training OD, as the natural tendency for most of us hardheaded, overachieving Americans is to think more is better and have a "charge the hills" attitude. OD training requires us to take the hills in stride and slow down in order to maintain the low intensity, even if this means walking up the hills.

Up/Vertical Intervals

This brand of Interval training follows the same time and intensity format as the Intervals described earlier. Vertical Intervals are just like other Intervals except for the terrain: Instead of being flat, it's moderate to very steep uphill. Because the body faces the extra battle against the force of gravity, these workouts increase strength, muscular endurance, and aerobic endurance all at once and recruit and condition the muscle fibers used in climbing (Figure 4.7).

Figure 4.7 Up/Vertical workouts are hard efforts, designed to train the body to adapt to the hills. Hill-bounding with poles up a steep slope is a favorite among cross-country skiers.

Given that almost everyone will encounter a hill or two in training and racing (if you live in Vermont, you'll have trouble finding a flat section), the benefits of hill training are many. First, the specificity principle becomes especially self-evident as the body makes the necessary physiological adaptations.

The psychological factor of doing hills is probably even more crucial. Every time I do Vertical Intervals with my buddy, we seem to find the toughest hills. We usually play a little game with ourselves during the workout. At an unspoken cue, one will push the other by slightly picking up the tempo as we crest the hill. This way, we actually increase our speed over the top of the hill. As we cruise down the other side, he'll always say how much he loves those hills, and I concur at what delightful little training gems they are and how lucky we are to be living in Vermont so that we can mine those gems each week. This training is perhaps the most rewarding of all. Sure, we get tired, but the psychological lift is surpassed only by race days. The feelings of accomplishment, confidence, and greater self-esteem are tremendous. Every hill presents a new challenge, a new dimension in our ability to handle the odds against us. One gains mental toughness from Vertical training sessions. Like Intervals, they are valuable for many reasons.

Strength

Strength is the ability of the muscle to exert force. Maximal strength is the maximal amount of force the muscle is able to exert in a single contraction. All endurance sports require strength, with the amount varying for each sport. How much is necessary for optimal performance? I think the answer rests with each individual athlete as well as with the technical requirements of the sport. Perhaps a better way to answer this question is to ask others and explore the answers. What happens to the body when we properly train for strength? What are the best ways to improve strength?

Proper Strength training elicits some interesting changes in the muscles. I mentioned muscle fibers earlier. It seems that each fiber has a portion that generates tension. This is composed of the contractile proteins of the muscle fiber called actin and myosin. Strength training increases the amount of actin and myosin in the fiber so that the fiber can generate a greater force. Interestingly, fast-twitch fibers have a greater potential for increasing the contractile proteins than slow-twitch fibers have. Conversely, slow-twitch fibers have more mitochondria (the aerobic powerhouses of the cell) than do fast-twitch fibers. Ironically, endurance training leads to a drop in contractile proteins in the fiber, whereas Strength training causes a decline in the endurance characteristics. Therefore, if you train only for endurance or only for strength, you may experience a loss of one or the other. (It's not suprising to me. When I lay off the strength routine, I notice my shirts fitting a bit looser due to the muscle atrophy resulting from disuse.)

Specificity training leads to specific changes in the body, changes related to the particular exercise or training used. Endurance training leads to increases in the size and number of mitochondria in the cell and the enzymes necessary for the aerobic energy process. Speed training improves the neuromuscular pathways and the energy supplies of the muscle fibers. Strength training improves the amount of contractile proteins, actin and myosin, in the fibers. Thus, each type of training stimulates particular adaptations of the muscle fibers.

Strength training can be either nonspecific or sport-specific. Nonspecific Strength training involves conditioning the muscles, tendons, and ligaments by using motions that do not exactly duplicate those used in competition. This would include weight training with machines or free weights and an assortment of calisthenics. Specific Strength training involves conditioning the muscles, tendons, and ligaments by using motions that closely or exactly duplicate those used in the sport (Figure 4.8). These would include a variety of methods, depending on the sport. Swimmers commonly use isokinetic swim benches. Cross-country skiers use rollerboard devices to duplicate double-poling technique. Cyclists ride up hills using hard gears. Rock climbers do fingertip chin-ups on doorjambs.

In general, it is a good idea to incorporate both nonspecific and specific Strength training into the training plan. As the competition season nears, more specific (versus nonspecific) Strength training should be used. Depending on your strength, about 20% of total training time during the Base stage, 10% to 15% during the Intensity stage, and 5% during Peak and Racing stages will be devoted to Strength training.

Regardless of the types of machines, calisthenics, or other Strength exercises you use, it is recommended that endurance athletes use a high-repetition, low-resistance method for all Strength training. For example, with weight machines, choose a weight you can lift 20 to 25 times per set instead of the typical 8 to 12 repetitions often suggested by manufacturers. Calisthenic routines should involve doing many repetitions and gradually improving the number over the weeks. For example, build up from doing 1 pull-up to 10 over the course of 20 weeks. Several types of Strength routines described in Appendix C offer advice on how to properly train for your sport.

Figure 4.8 The author demonstrates ski-specific strength training using the Väsa Trainer (photo courtesy Väsa, Inc., Williston, Vermont).

It is important to emphasize sport-specific Strength training if you have the facilities or creativity to do so. Two interesting stories describe how important sport-specific strength is to some elite endurance athletes. Elite biathlete and cross-country skier Josh Thompson has gained a reputation for his superb Strength workouts. On a recent trip to the Dachstein Glacier in Austria, he impressed people with several workouts that involved double-poling on roller skis up a paved road, called the Dachsteinstrasse, that steadily climbs 1000 meters vertical in only 5 kilometers—a 20% grade. He didn't even use his legs to propel him up the hill, only his upper body for poling. He said, "I want to be ridiculously strong."

Greg Varney, a national-class canoe racer, is also a real Maine lumberjack. He wields a 25-pound chainsaw like I use my pen. One summer while I was visiting, I asked him whether he would join me for a weight-training session at the gym. He thought for a minute, scratched his whiskers, and replied, "It seems to me that those guys that lift weights aren't all that strong. Sure, they have big muscles, but I have yet to see one who can keep up with me on the river. Their muscles are built on—mine are built in."

An Effective Translator

It is essential that endurance athletes and coaches understand each other. Systematic training provides a way to identify the time, intensity, and, ultimately, the physiological purpose for every type of workout. The SERIOUS acronym defines the various training components in order to further the understanding and interpretation of the many methods for completing training workouts. Chapter 5 provides a detailed description of the intensity levels appropriate for each of the SERIOUS training components. In chapter 6 you will learn how to create a systematic training plan.

TRAINING INTENSITY

A n essential ingredient of the systematic approach to training is intensity. Every workout has a distinct physiological purpose, and the time and intensity of the training session are directly linked to this purpose. Specifically, each component of SERIOUS training is assigned an intensity level at which that component should be completed. This allows you to implement a checks-and-balance system for controlling the stress level of a workout by checking the purpose of the component against the time allotment and intensity assignment of the session, then adjusting as needed.

In this chapter the following components of intensity are described in relation to the systematic approach:

- The physiological characteristics of intensity levels
- The intensity level for each SERIOUS component
- How to determine specific intensity levels
- Methods for monitoring intensity

Physiological Characteristics of Intensity Levels

Intensity may be described in terms of kilocalories burned per minute, the percentage of one's maximal oxygen uptake capacity ($\dot{V}O_2$max), or heart rate level. Oxygen uptake is considered the standard for measuring the physiological stress of exercise. In endurance sports, success is in large part dependent on the body's oxygen uptake ability. The more oxygen that can be delivered to the working muscles, the greater the energy supply, and the faster the body can travel over distance.

Exercise science has determined that specific training adaptations are achieved when you exercise at various intensities as related to percentages of $\dot{V}O_2$max. However, oxygen uptake capacity must be measured in the laboratory with expensive equipment and by qualified professionals to which few of us have ready access. Fortunately, research has shown a reliable relationship between oxygen consumption and heart rate (beats per minute) for monitoring intensity during training. The method for calculating intensity levels by heart rate, described later in this chapter, produces results that for the most part accurately correspond with relative percentages of $\dot{V}O_2$max.

The physiological effects of various training intensities dictate the overall training plan with respect to the amount of each training component scheduled during a given training cycle. For example, low-intensity training sessions (such as Overdistance) are most effective if the intensity is between 55% and 65% $\dot{V}O_2$max; this develops aerobic energy pathways and improves capillary density in muscle tissue, proliferation of muscle cell mitochondria, oxidative enzyme activity, and fat substrate mobilization and utilization in the muscle cells. Concurrently, Intervals, Up/Vertical Intervals, and Race/Pace sessions, when planned appropriately, are best accomplished at an intensity at or slightly below the anaerobic threshold (AT) in order to improve aerobic energy pathways, the oxygen transport system, the ability of the body to remove lactic acid from the muscles, and the recruitment of more muscle fibers, particularly the fast oxydative glycolytic (FOG) fibers not normally used in Overdistance training.

The Five Intensity Levels

Each component of systematic training, as described by the SERIOUS model or by your own descriptions of training components, must be accomplished at a designated intensity. Changing the intensity specified for a given workout will alter the purpose of the session and, more profoundly, will affect the overall pattern of the training plan. Many endurance athletes tend to train at medium to high intensity for a large percentage of the training volume. This is due to a poor understanding of the specific purposes of training components and their appropriate intensities.

As each workout maintains its own personality, the level of intensity will be an integral factor in determining that personality. Use the following descriptions of the five levels of intensity as guidelines for application to your own training situation. Table 5.1 illustrates the physiological adaptations that occur at various training intensities and the corresponding SERIOUS training components.

Level I
(55%-65% $\dot{V}O_2$max
or 60%-70% Maximum Heart Rate [MHR])

Overdistance workouts will be accomplished at this level. Although the effort may seem ridiculously easy at first, it is essential to maintain close control and complete this training within the zone. In the end, the effort, because it is longer than other types of training, will be quite fatiguing due to energy and fluid losses. For these reasons, Overdistance workouts lasting over 90 minutes should be considered high-stress sessions, despite the low intensity. Most Strength workouts will elicit heart rates at this level as well, depending on the exercises and the tempo at which they are performed.

Level II
(66%-75% $\dot{V}O_2$max or 71%-75% MHR)

Endurance and easy Speed workouts (except during Peak and Racing stages) will be done at Level II intensity. The feel is slightly harder than OD but must not exceed the limits. Level II intensity is probably the level at which the vast majority of people train day in and day out. Although this certainly has a positive training effect, especially with untrained or beginning exercisers, we find that for serious endurance athletes, too much training at this intensity precludes optimal adaptation needed from training at Level I intensity (as described in chapter 4).

Level III
(76%-80% $\dot{V}O_2$max or 76%-80% MHR)

Typically, very little training should take place in this intensity zone. Some endurance work may be done at this level. Longer races will most likely be accomplished in this intensity zone, depending on your fitness and the terrain of the course. Much depends your anaerobic threshold as expressed as a percentage of $\dot{V}O_2$max. If your threshold

Table 5.1

Physiological Adaptations to Various Training Intensities

Level	% $\dot{V}O_2$max	% Maximum heart rate	Physiological adaptations ($\uparrow$ = improves or increases)	SERIOUS components or workouts used at intensity levels
I	55-65	60-70	$\uparrow$ Aerobic energy sources $\uparrow$ Aerobic energy pathways $\uparrow$ Capillary density $\uparrow$ Mitochondria proliferation $\uparrow$ Free fatty acid mobilization	Overdistance, Strength
II	66-75	71-75	$\uparrow$ Aerobic energy sources $\uparrow$ Aerobic energy pathways	Endurance, Strength, Body Speeds
III	76-80	76-80	$\uparrow$ Aerobic energy pathways $\uparrow$ Recruitment of FOG fibers $\uparrow$ Aerobic glycolysis $\uparrow$ Oxygen transport system	Endurance, Strength
IV	81-90	81-90	$\uparrow$ Aerobic energy pathways $\uparrow$ Anaerobic energy pathways $\uparrow$ Recruitment of FOG fibers $\uparrow$ Anaerobic threshold (AT) $\uparrow$ Oxygen transport system $\uparrow$ Lactic acid clearance	Intervals, Up/Vertical, Race/Pace
V	91-100	91-100	$\uparrow$ Anaerobic energy sources $\uparrow$ Fast-twitch FG fiber recruitment $\uparrow$ Speed and neuromuscular coordination	Racing, Peaking Speeds

is low and falls in this range, then Interval, Vertical, and Race/Pace work will be accomplished at this level until the AT becomes higher.

Level III intensity is lower than Race/Pace, but harder than OD, intensity. Therefore, too much training at Level III may prove ineffective for increasing $\dot{V}O_2$max but nevertheless drain precious glycogen stores because the main fuel substrate at this intensity is glycogen.

Level IV
(81%-90% $\dot{V}O_2$max or 81%-90% MHR)

Intervals, Vertical training, and Race/Pace sessions require a Level IV intensity, which is also called anaerobic threshold training. Training at this intensity will improve the body's ability to transport oxygen, increase the recruitment of fast oxidative glycolytic (FOG) muscle fibers, and improve both aerobic and anaerobic energy pathways.

These workouts will require you to "tune in" to the physiological cues that indicate that level of work that elicits the threshold between aerobic and anaerobic effort. Anyone who has run hill intervals will have experienced the "rubbery legs" syndrome. Scientists are still arguing about what to call this physiological state. The popular expression used over the last decade has been "crossing the anaerobic threshold." It is the point at which lactic acid accumulation reaches concentrations where it limits performance and is fatiguing. All skeletal muscles have a lactic acid accumulation threshold—a point beyond which the muscle cells can no longer effectively process the lactate being produced. Generally, this point occurs at high intensities for well-trained endurance athletes. The lactate, or metabolic waste, quickly accumulates in the muscle cells and then enters the bloodstream. If the accumulation becomes too great, the muscles will fail to contract efficiently, and exercise will slow considerably until recovery is allowed.

Training at or slightly below the AT usually results in the ability of the body to buffer or recycle lactate during high-intensity work. Elite endurance athletes are likely to have high ATs, that is, they can sustain high-intensity exercise for a long period of time before fatiguing. Later in this chapter, I will discuss the AT in greater detail, including some of the current methods for determining when it occurs.

Level V
(91%-100% $\dot{V}O_2$max or 91%-100% MHR)

Only during the Peaking and Racing stages will Level V work be included in the training program. This type of training stimulates anaerobic energy pathways, fast-twitch muscle fibers, and improves anaerobic energy supplies and speed. During a peaking or tapering stage, it will be used only in Peaking Speed sessions. Basically, these Speed sessions will involve all-out sprints for 15 to 20 seconds, followed by 15 to 20 seconds of easy recovery. The sequence is repeated for the length designated for the session. These workouts will be very difficult but will sharpen muscle efficiency and neuromuscular coordination at maximum speed and will boost the anaerobic and aerobic energy systems. When the first races arrive, your body will be in top condition.

Determining the Intensity Levels

There are several methods for monitoring the five levels of intensity used in SERIOUS training. Heart rate is perhaps the most widely known method, but it has been my experience that many advanced endurance athletes rely on heart rate as just one objective marker of intensity. Most also use a combination of physiological and psychological cues for monitoring intensity. Such cues include ventilatory (breathing) rate and exertion, perceived exertion, and other bodily cues such as the feel of the muscles, the throbbing of blood in the ears, coordination, and the level of fatigue.

Since the development of sophisticated, wireless heart monitors, such as the model shown in Figure 5.1, many top endurance athletes are using heart rate monitoring in conjunction with subjective feelings to judge proper intensity levels. One can directly measure or estimate appropriate percentages of $\dot{V}O_2$max and the heart rate zones associated with those levels and then use the heart rate levels in training, measuring precisely with the heart monitor. This eliminates the guesswork from specific training components and the intensity levels for each. These monitors also offer fantastic opportunities for biofeedback regarding intensity for various activities performed in any terrain and environmental condition.

Most successful athletes are extraordinary when it comes to listening to their bodies' intensity cues. Years of trial and error have enabled them to fine-tune their response to each intensity level. Conversely, the majority of endurance athletes do not have a good handle on the levels of intensity required for each component of SERIOUS, especially athletes with the ''bull in the china shop'' approach to training. As with any refined craft, this takes either a very special talent or a dedication to shaping a rough concept into a fine work of art. Therefore, monitoring heart rate can be an effective tool for refining your ability to feel each level of intensity. It takes practice, and some will learn faster than others. The key is that eventually you will possess an entire repertoire of cues for detecting the intensity level of every

Figure 5.1 Heart monitors that utilize a wireless telemetry transmission are as accurate as an electrocardiogram.

training session. As runner and skier Skip Hamilton says, "I never realized that Overdistance intensity training should be so low. It's become guilt-producing easy, even though I get tired enough over the long run."

Heart Rate: The Foundation of Intensity

Consider your heart for a moment. It's the hub of most functions at rest and at exercise. It gets messages from the control center in your brain telling it to speed up or slow down its pumping action. If your muscles need more fuel and oxygen, the heart is stimulated to pump more blood to the needy muscle cells. If it's time to rest or recover, the messages tell it to slow down. The process is an autonomic response—in other words, the body will do this automatically. Luckily, we don't have to think about it too much.

However, when conditioning the body, coaxing it into a higher level of fitness, you can use heart rate as a monitor of the intensity at which you are asking your body to perform. Consider the components of your training. Each objective—Speed, Endurance, Race/Pace, and so on—needs to be performed at a certain intensity for you to achieve maximum benefit from the workout. Therefore, measuring heart rate will quantify and ultimately optimize the conditioning response of your training sessions. The following sections will teach you how to check heart rate and give you a system for calculating training heart rate (THR) levels of your own. You will be able to individualize and control the intensity of your training plan by using heart rate.

Calculating the Five Heart Rate Intensity Levels

There are several methods for calculating the THR intensity levels. Some are more accurate than others, and some are more convenient than others. The following methods are the most widely accepted by sport scientists and coaches.

Maximal Oxygen Uptake Capacity ($\dot{V}O_2max$)

The best way to determine training levels is to have a maximal stress test administered by a qualified professional such as a sport physiologist, sports medicine physician, or cardiologist. If you are over 35 years old or have a family history of heart disease, it is highly recommended that you take such a test annually, especially before partaking in strenuous exercise or before beginning to exercise after a layoff from regular physical activity.

Typically, two physiological measurements will be taken. First, your maximum heart rate (MHR), the maximum number of beats your heart can make in one minute, will be measured. Along with the MHR, the health status of your heart will be monitored and assessed for signs of heart disease. This is a valuable preventative health measure. Many stress tests are administered with consideration only to maximum heart rate and heart health status. While this is useful, it does not tell the entire story, which can be discovered with the second measurement, $\dot{V}O_2max$ (Figure 5.2).

If you can take a stress test and have $\dot{V}O_2max$ measured directly, you'll be able to determine training heart rate levels as a function of a percentage of $\dot{V}O_2max$. After all, the main theme of training systematically for endurance sports is to raise your oxygen uptake capacity. Given that each training component in the SERIOUS model has a specific physiological purpose, it is useful to know the relative percentage of $\dot{V}O_2$max and corresponding heart rate for each component. If you do have a stress test to measure $\dot{V}O_2$max directly, use the following steps to determine training heart rate levels:

Figure 5.2 Maximal oxygen uptake test for determining $\dot{V}O_2$max and heart rate maximum.

Step 1. Determine $\dot{V}O_2$max value (usually expressed in milliliters per kilogram per minute [ml/kg/min]).

Step 2. Multiply the $\dot{V}O_2$max by the percentages given for each level as follows:

LEVEL 1: 55%-65% (or .55 × $\dot{V}O_2$max; .65 × $\dot{V}O_2$max)
LEVEL 2: 66%-75%
LEVEL 3: 76%-80%
LEVEL 4: 81%-90% (The anaerobic threshold will usually be in this level, but it varies.)
LEVEL 5: 91%-100%

For example, if $\dot{V}O_2$max is 66 ml/kg/min, then Level I $\dot{V}O_2$ value will range between 36.3 ml/kg/min (55%) and 42.9 ml/kg/min (65%).

Step 3.   For each $\dot{V}O_2$ level, look at the test data for the heart rate values you had during the test and determine the actual heart rate values you experienced at each $\dot{V}O_2$ level. For example, if at 55% $\dot{V}O_2$max (36.3 ml/kg/min in the example in Step 2) the heart rate was 136 beats per minute (bpm), then 136 bpm will serve as the lower limit for Level I training.

One bit of caution regarding $\dot{V}O_2$max tests. There are many types of oxygen uptake analyzing systems as well as other variables that can affect the results of a $\dot{V}O_2$max test. If you use this method, try to compare your results over time if you can get tested 2 to 4 times (or at least once) per year. However, comparing your test results to those of other people who are tested on other equipment by different professionals can be misleading.

Calculating THR by the Karvonen Method

Calculation of the five training heart rate levels using the Karvonen method is one of the most common approaches used today. It was developed by taking real test data from many $\dot{V}O_2$max tests and creating a formula that produced heart rate levels that matched the real data quite accurately. Table 5.2 provides a summary worksheet approach to calculating the five levels of intensity with the Karvonen method.

Step 1.   Determine maximum heart rate (MHR). The Karvonen method is dependent upon knowing your true MHR. There are a couple of ways to find your true MHR:

1. The best way to find true MHR is to take an exercise stress test on a treadmill or bicycle ergometer while being monitored with an electrocardiogram as described above. This is also the safest way. You'll also benefit by learning about the health status of your heart. If you do not have $\dot{V}O_2$max measured, then at least you can get your true MHR.
2. If you are positive that you are in good condition, you can do the 1½-mile run test. *Do not attempt this if you are over 35 and have not had a thorough physical exam with a stress test, or if you are in poor condition.* This test involves running 1½ miles as fast as you can over a fairly level course. Warm up and stretch well before the test. Good pacing and motivation are necessary for you to do well. Time your run and use it as a reference later in your program. During the last quarter-mile of the run, go

all out. At the finish, stop and count your heart rate immediately. This will be your MHR. A helpful tool for this test is a good pulse monitor, which affords you accuracy and ease of measurement.

3. Probably the easiest method of calculating MHR is simply subtracting your age from 220: 220 − age = estimated MHR. Although I have seen variations between a person's true MHR and the estimated MHR, this method is still useful. Minor adjustments in the five calculated levels of training heart rate will help compensate for error. If the training level seems too hard or too easy, make the appropriate adjustments.

Step 2.   The next measure you'll need before calculating the five training levels is your true resting heart rate. This is done by counting your pulse for a full minute, first thing in the morning, preferably BEFORE you get out of bed. Do this for five mornings and make an average. (NOTE: You may need to void before taking a morning pulse. A full bladder can slightly elevate resting heart rate.)

Step 3.   Now you're ready to calculate the five levels of training heart rate. Use the formula in Table 5.2 for figuring each level. Figure 5.3 illustrates the various training zones as calculated by the Karvonen method. You can use this graph to determine your heart rate zones.

Level IV Intensity: The Anaerobic Threshold

Much controversy exists concerning the value of and the methods for determining the anaerobic threshold (AT). One way to measure the AT is in a physiology laboratory, with blood tests taken at frequent intervals during ever-increasing work intensity. The Soviet Bloc and some Western European countries have been using the lactate test for years to determine ATs for their athletes and to adjust training according to these values. However, in the United States, lactate testing has not been widely used to monitor and train athletes on a daily basis. Blood lactate testing is available primarily to elite athletes.

Another method popular with physiologists has been to measure ventilation during a maximal stress test for VO_2max. It has been suggested that the AT occurs when there is a break in the ventilation curve relative to oxygen consumed. However, most of us need to rely on some other method for testing the AT. For years, athletes have relied on subjective feel for determining this threshold. Some athletes can do well with this method and will train Intervals, Vertical, and Race/Pace workouts at or slightly below the AT intensity.

However, Conconi, Ferrari, Ziglio, Droghetti, and Codeca (1982) indicate that there are field tests that are easy to do and are noninvasive (no blood samples) for determining the AT and the heart rate at which the AT occurs. Dr. Conconi developed what is now referred to as the Test Conconi for cyclists, runners, cross-country skiers, and swimmers. Basically, the test involves a series of repeated intervals of gradually increasing intensity over a set distance and course. Heart rate for the last quarter of the interval and the speed of the interval are recorded and plotted. The AT is said to exist at that point where the line between speed and heart rate deflects, creating a "knee" in the graph. By performing this test periodically, say, every 2 to 3 weeks, one can determine the heart rate at AT. Once AT is determined, all Interval, Vertical, and Race/Pace training should take place within a range 10% below the AT heart rate.

Cyclists have used the Test Conconi with great success over the last few years. In January 1984 Francesco Moser broke the world hour-cycling record twice in one week. He had trained using the Test Conconi. The Italian foursome who won the 1984 Olympic 100-kilometer time trial, setting Olympic and world records, used the Test Conconi to prepare for that race. Runners and cross-country skiers are beginning to use the method in the field. I think that it has merit but must be applied with prudence and with a scientific approach that considers environmental factors such as wind, temperature, humidity, and surface used, all of which must be exactly the same for each test. I have modified the Test Conconi and have used it successfully with many athletes. Appendix E gives detailed instructions on how to perform this test.

Table 5.2

Intensity Levels Calculated by Heart Rate

The method for calculating heart rate intensity levels is based on the Karvonen method. These are estimates and may need some adjustments based on the subjective feeling you have during workouts. Please see the section "The Five Intensity Levels" in this chapter for an explanation of the appropriate intensities for various training components.

How to Calculate Your Training Heart Rate Levels

1. Determine your maximum heart rate (MHR), either by maximum treadmill stress test with your physician, or by estimating it with the formula: MHR = 220 − age.   (Cont.)

Table 5.2 (Continued)

2. Subtract your resting heart rate (taken for 1 minute, first thing in A.M.) from MHR to obtain adjusted MHR.
3. Multiply adjusted MHR by intensity level percentage (e.g., 60%)
4. Add resting heart rate back to result of step 3. This now will represent the intensity level heart rate for the percentage selected in step 3.

Example For 30-Year-Old

1. 220 − 30 = 190 bpm (estimated MHR)
2. 190 − 55 bpm (resulting pulse) = 135 (adjusted max)
3. 135 × .60 (for 60% - Level I Intensity) = 81
4. 81 + 55 (resting pulse) = 136

136 bpm = 60% max to be used as lower limit of Level I intensity workouts.

Intensity Levels for Systematic Training			
Level	Heart rate percentage	Actual heart rates	SERIOUS components
I	60-70%	_____ - _____	Overdistance, Strength
II	71-75%	_____ - _____	Endurance, Strength, Speed
III	76-80%	_____ - _____	Endurance, Strength
IV	81-90%	_____ - _____	Intervals, Up, Race/Pace
V	91-100%	_____ - _____	Racing, Peaking

Subjective Methods for Monitoring Intensity

Essential in developing a systematic training plan is incorporation of the correct amount of Level IV, or threshold, training. The training plan templates for SERIOUS training presented in Appendix A incorporate the recommended amounts of Interval, Vertical, and Race/Pace workouts for a gradual buildup from the aerobic Base stage

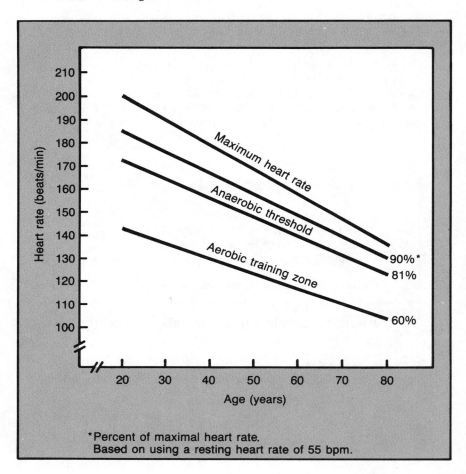

Figure 5.3 Heart rate training zones, calculated with Karvonen method.

through the Intensity stage. The key to successful training at Level IV intensities is to cue in to the body's signals for lactate accumulation.

Although not conclusively documented, ventilation, your rate and depth of breathing, can be an effective cue for AT. Generally, when you are at the AT, breathing will become markedly more rapid. This is associated with increased anaerobic energy metabolism. The by-product of this increase is greater lactic acid, production. The body tries to eliminate lactic acid, and the result is an increase in carbon dioxide production. Carbon dioxide is not tolerated in the system, so the body does everything it can to eliminate it. Your breathing increases to "blow off" CO_2 as fast as possible (It is the increased CO_2 production that causes the breathing changes, not a need to get more oxygen into the system). When you feel your breathing change from deep and rhythmical to a significantly increased frequency, ease off on the throttle and try to maintain an effort slightly below the one that caused the change in ventilation. Figure 5.4 illustrates this phenomenon.

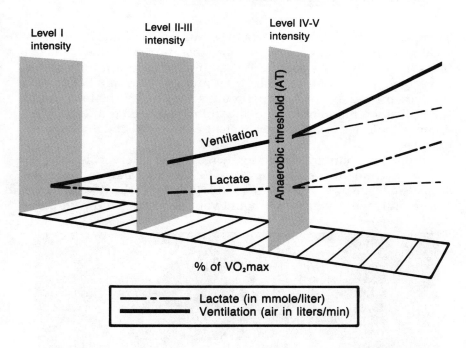

Figure 5.4 Ventilation and lactic acid changes at the anaerobic threshold. As intensity increases, more fast-twitch muscle fibers are recruited.

Another way to detect the AT is with cues from the muscles. Reduction in coordination, rubbery feelings, or burning are all signs of working above the AT. Again, tune in to this feeling and the heart rate associated with it and reduce the intensity accordingly. However, reliability of these cues is questionable, and I'm sure there is considerable variation between athletes.

Because endurance athletes traditionally train too much of the time at or above the AT, I recommend conservatism be exercised with all Level IV training. It is best to train about 5 to 10 heart beats per minute below the AT heart rate for most Level IV training. When the Peak stage comes, it will not take long to fine-tune your body for racing. Premature high-intensity training will likely lead to an early peak, if one is achieved at all.

Monitoring Training Heart Rate

The most common and least expensive way to check heart rate is by feeling the pulse in an artery on your wrist, throat, or under the left breast (Figure 5.5). As soon as you stop moving, count the number of beats you feel in 10 seconds, then multiply that number by 6 to give you the number of beats per minute. At rest, it is better to count the beats for a full minute. The only thing you need is a watch with seconds indicated. Digital sport watches work well and are fairly inexpensive.

If you are counting heart rate by feeling an artery, it is most accurate to count the beats for only 10 seconds and multiply the 10-second value by 6. The reason for this is that your body will recover very rapidly when you stop to count your heart rate, and your pulse

Figure 5.5 Measuring the heart rate manually.

will drop significantly within 1 minute. Therefore, you will not obtain a true representation of exercise heart rate if you count for more than 10 seconds.

You may have trouble feeling your pulse or being able to count the beats at high heart rates. It takes practice before you gain a good feel for pulse taking. Modern technology has taken the guesswork out of heart rate monitoring for us. Scientists have developed some very accurate electronic pulse monitors that are available on the market. Most elite endurance athletes are using these devices regularly to monitor training. If you are interested in precision as well as the ability to record your pulse throughout the workout and then play it back, these training aids are for you. My personal experience has led me to believe that these heart monitors are "the best thing since sliced bread" for the endurance athlete. I feel that every developing athlete should have access to one regularly in training. The opportunities to learn about various intensity levels as related to a well-planned, systematic training program are great.

Variation in the Training Heart Rate With Different Sports

Heart rate is not always the best measure of oxygen uptake and training effect. There can be significant differences in the pulse rate response to a given workload or oxygen consumption relative to $\dot{V}O_2$max. It has been shown that with arm work alone, such as with double-poling in cross-country skiing, you cannot obtain the same $\dot{V}O_2$max that you can reach with running, despite the fact that your pulse can reach the maximum in both cases. The probable reason for this is that less muscle mass is engaged in arm work than in leg work, so the oxygen demand is ultimately less as well. Thus, in the case of the cross-country skier, a greater training effect will be gained by running, diagonal, or freestyle skiing, which engages more muscle mass and creates a greater load on the system than does double-poling at the same heart rate.

Additionally, it is thought that $\dot{V}O_2$max values vary according to training specificity. Tests have shown that trained triathletes achieve their highest $\dot{V}O_2$max scores while running, with $\dot{V}O_2$max scores for cycling and swimming at 95.7% and 86.8% of the running $\dot{V}O_2$max, respectively. Other tests have shown that untrained subjects also achieve their highest $\dot{V}O_2$max values in running, with cycling $\dot{V}O_2$max typically 8% to 12% lower and swimming $\dot{V}O_2$max 18% to 22% lower than running $\dot{V}O_2$max values. Conversely, highly trained cyclists' cycling $\dot{V}O_2$max values have tested approximately equal to their running scores and highly trained swimmers achieved 94% of their running $\dot{V}O_2$max scores while swimming.

Training heart rate levels relative to percentages of $\dot{V}O_2$max as calculated with the Karvonen method seem to be most accurate for running and may need adjustment depending on the level of training, the sport, or the training method. Unfortunately, it is unclear how much adjustment is necessary. Experimentation using pulse monitors and subjective feelings will help you determine training zone adjustments for various activities.

Adaptation

As your body adapts to training, so will your heart rate response for a given workout. For example, during Week 1 of your program, you may run 3 miles in 21 minutes at a Level I heart rate. Twelve weeks later, you probably will be able to run that same 3-mile course in less time at the same heart rate. Your body will have adjusted to the demands of your training program.

Monitoring your training heart rate levels regularly will lead to a finely tuned sense of your body and its response to various exercise demands. It does not take long before you will gain a fairly accurate feel for the various levels of exertion. The more you know about your body, the better you'll be able to deal with the stresses of training.

Resting Heart Rate

Resting heart rate, or morning pulse, serves as a good indicator of your state of training. Typically, morning pulse will decrease as your level of fitness increases. Mine dips as low as 36 when I'm in super shape. One friend on the U.S. biathlon team has recorded his at 29 beats per minute! Resting pulse is not the only indicator of fitness—there are too many other variables affecting it. However, monitoring morning pulse on a daily basis can be very useful. I recommend that you record it in your training log so that you can refer to it later.

A rise in morning pulse of 10% above average can mean one of several things regarding your training. You may be coming down with a cold, the flu, or another ailment. Other times it may mean that your hard, Level IV workout yesterday was a bit too much. Emotional stress, lack of sleep, or jet lag can all elevate the morning pulse. In each case, the body is responding to the demand by requiring more rest. The best remedy for elevated morning pulse is rest, rest, and more rest. You needn't fear losing a conditioning benefit by missing the workout scheduled for the day. You'll do much better to take the day off and pick up the training plan on the next scheduled workout. Chapter 7 covers the SERIOUS system training log, including a complete description of monitoring a variety of stress factors that affect training and recovery.

Environmental Factors and Heart Rate

Some environmental conditions will affect both morning and training pulse. Training in the heat puts a greater stress on the cardiovascular system as the body struggles to keep the cooling mechanism working properly. Therefore, training in the heat reduces the value of heart rate as a good training monitor.

Hypohydration, or lack of adequate fluids, will cause the heart rate to soar above normal. Be sure to stay well hydrated before, during, and after training.

Altitude also affects heart rate. The first 2 or 3 weeks of training at high altitude will be accompanied by higher heart rates for given workout intensities, after which this effect on the body usually goes away. I recommend that you back off on training times and intensities, get plenty of rest, and consume plenty of fluids whenever you go to high altitude.

CREATING A SYSTEMATIC TRAINING PLAN: A WORKSHEET APPROACH

N ow you are ready to create your own systematic training plan, using a step-by-step process. The information presented in chapters 1 through 5 were intended to provide the foundation for the planning phase presented here. In this chapter, you will

- outline the objectives of your training plan;
- determine how many hours you will train and the character of each training cycle;
- determine the percentage of various training components per cycle; and
- create systematic training plans using a simple format, including determination of the weekly training pattern and intensity levels.

Getting Started

You'll need some tools to make your job a bit easier (Figure 6.1). First, you will need a calculator (a scientific calculator is best because it reads minutes, but you can use a standard calculator and work to fractions of an hour, finally converting fractions of an hour to minutes by multiplying the fraction by 60—example: 1.25 hours = 75 minutes). Second, you will need a pencil with an eraser. If you try to use an ink pen, you may find it frustrating when you make mistakes! You'll need to refer to the blank worksheets presented in Appendix A, which correspond to the sample worksheets used in this chapter. You'll find it extremely useful to have access to a photocopy machine to duplicate the Appendix A blank worksheet forms before you start working on your plan. It will be necessary to copy all of your master worksheets after you have finished your planning, also, so you can refer to them later or in case of loss.

Figure 6.1 It's fun to plan your own training program.

Using the Master Templates

The master templates of Worksheet 6.4 in Appendix B can serve either as guides or as gospel for your particular situation. All you'll have to do is determine your Year Hours and plug in the appropriate percentage of your total Year Hours as indicated in the template. These are plans I have created based on much experience working with many top athletes in developing their training plans. These master template programs have been carefully developed to suit typical situations, such as training for a 10K road race, a middle-distance triathlon, or a cross-country ski marathon. However, I encourage you to go through the planning process outlined in this chapter, even if you use one of the master templates, so that you will gain a solid understanding of the physiological principles of systematic training. If you use a template from Appendix B, most of the work in Worksheets 6.2, 6.3, and 6.4 will have been done for you. You will still need to determine

- your objectives for the overall plan (Worksheet 6.1);
- your Year Hours, actual dates of the 4-week cycles, and the training stage and emphasis of each cycle (Steps 1, 2, and 3 of Worksheet 6.2); and
- your weekly pattern and daily workouts for each 4-week cycle (Worksheet 6.5).
- Let's get started! NOTE: As you work through the planning process, remember to refer to the sample worksheets provided to give you ideas for your own plan.

Worksheet 6.1: Objectives of the Overall Plan

Put a lot of thought into this step. If you can become quite clear about your goals, your motivations for training, and your strengths and weaknesses at the outset, the rest of your planning process will flow smoothly. Refer to chapter 2 for more guidance in setting these objectives.

1 Step 1: Events and Competitions

Write out the actual race distances you will be training to compete in during the year. You may also want to write down certain fitness events or challenges you are planning. For example, you may be creating a plan for summer triathlons but also want to participate in cross-country ski marathon in winter.

2 Step 2: Performance Goals

Here you need to clarify actual performance objectives, including times and distances. Be realistic in your goal setting. Use past performances, your present fitness level determined with methods described in chapter 2, and a comparison of yourself to others to clearly mark a realistic level of expected achievement. It is also a good idea to set some short-term goals, such as completing a long Overdistance workout, keeping an up-to-date log, or competing in a few races for training.

3 Step 3: Physical Preparation

First, make an assessment of your physical strengths and weaknesses as related to the specific demands of your sport(s). Next, try to prioritize each of these, especially the areas where you need improvement. Identify the top three areas needing improvement and the top three strengths, then set these as primary objectives for your physical preparation. For example, if you know that aerobic endurance and strength are characteristics you need to improve, then a greater percentage of your training hours need to be planned to improve these areas. You will need to refer to these when you come to Worksheets 6.2 and 6.3.

4 Step 4: Psychological Preparation

 Using the process in Step 3, develop a clear idea of your psychological strengths and the areas that need more work, as well as a strategy for improving your mental game plan (see Terry Orlick's book, *Psyching For Sport*, 1986).

5 Step 5: Technical Preparation

This refers to actual technique used in training and competition. For example, if as a cyclist your climbing technique is inefficient, then you need to work on this during specific hill-climbing training workouts. Also, it is a good idea to refer to your training logs from years past, coaches, more experienced athletes, books, and videos for feedback and critique of your technical abilities.

6 Step 6: Tests and Standards

Physiological tests can be useful in assessing your progress throughout a training program. Determination of percent body fat diet analysis,

SAMPLE WORKSHEET 6.1:
Objectives of the overall year plan

Training plan for the year 19 <u>88-89</u>

Name   <u>Rob Sleamaker</u>

1 **Events and competitions** <u>Cross-country ski racing—10K-25K distances,</u>
<u>10K biathlon</u>

2	Performance goals	35-minute 10K, 91-minute 25K, 38-minute 10K, biathlon

Finish a 50K race comfortably. |
3	Physical preparation	Improve overall aerobic capacity; increase ski-specific strength; identify and train with the anaerobic threshold during Intervals and Race/Pace workouts; work on a good restoration routine to include massage, relaxation, fluids, and high-carbohydrate diet.
4	Psychological preparation	Develop solid pre-race routine; improve mental imagery skills; increase self-confidence; practice relaxation exercises.
5	Technical preparation	Correct body position while double poling; efficient stride length; relaxed but fast tempo; improved balance. Work on skis to get them fast.
6	Tests & standards	General physical exam in May; blood testing every three months; VO_2max tests every 3 months; body fat test every 3 months; Conconi test for AT every month after August.

treadmill stress testing for maximum heart rate and V̇O₂max, and blood testing can all be very helpful if the information is accurate and if a qualified professional, such as a sports medicine physician, administers the tests and interprets the results for you in relation to your program. Generally, the more serious an athlete you are, the more you need to incorporate these tests into your total program. However, you can use some simple performance tests to monitor your progress occasionally. Time trials over a set course can be very useful if conditions remain relatively constant from one trial to the next. Gradual fat weight loss can be detected with the bathroom scale or with a ''pinch an inch'' test with your thumb and forefinger.

Worksheet 6.2: The 4-Week Cycle's Character

This step will help you make informed decisions about the character or personality of each 4-week training cycle. It will be helpful if you have previous log records for reference. If not, do your best to remember how you have trained in the past. You'll find it useful to refer to Table 2.2 from chapter 2 to review the character of 4-week cycles.

1 Step 1: Total Year Hours

The number of hours (often referred to as total volume or Year Hours) you select for your plan is based on several important factors. If you have accurate records, then you can compare your Year Hours to those listed in Table 6.1. If you would like to add more volume to this year's program, you can typically be safe with a 5% to 10% increase over last year. Otherwise, refer to Table 2.3 in chapter 2 to determine the correct percentage of increase in training volume.

However, make increases only until your yearly volume reaches the highest levels listed for top athletes in your sport in Table 6.1. If you trained fewer than 400 hours last year and feel confident that you can handle a greater increase than 10%, you may want to try as much as a 20% increase in this year's volume. However, do this with extreme caution and be sure to follow many of the restoration principles described in chapter 11. Increasing your training volume too much can result in overtraining and illness and will have a negative effect on competition.

If you are like many working professionals, you may have a limited, set amount of time you can devote to training each week. In this case, determine your total Year Hours by multiplying your available training time per week by 52. For example, if you can devote 5

Table 6.1

Training Volumes for Endurance Sports

Level of competition	Hours per year				
	Running	Cycling	Triathlon	X-C ski	Rowing
World class	500-700	700-1200	800-1400	700-1000	700-1200
Top citizen	400-500	500-700	500-800	500-700	500-700
Good citizen	300-400	350-500	400-500	400-500	400-500
Average citizen	200-300	200-350	300-400	300-400	300-400
Beginner	<200	<200	<300	<300	<300

hours per week maximum to training, then your total Year Hours will be about 260 hours. You'll also need to keep this in mind when planning the percentage of total year volume per cycle and the periodization per cycle so that there is not undue variation from your schedule.

Another factor that needs consideration is the amount of time you will spend warming up and cooling down at Level I and II intensities. Typically, you might spend as much as 40 to 75 hours on warm-up and cool-down during the year. However, this is not specifically planned into the total time allotments for Speed, Interval, Up/Vertical, Race/Pace, and Strength workouts as presented in the master templates in Appendix B. You can approach this problem in one of two ways. First, and perhaps most desirable, keep Year Hours as planned and use part of the time allotments for Overdistance and Endurance training as warm-up and cool-down time for the other training components during the week. This approach works best if you have limited training time per week and probably can fit only one workout per day into the schedule. For example, plan a short, 30- to 45-minute Endurance workout on a day you are also planning a Strength workout; use the Endurance time as warm-up and cool-down for the Strength session. A moderate-length Overdistance workout of 60 minutes may enhance recovery if used directly after a stressful Interval or Race/Pace session.

If you are training seriously year-round, use the second approach for integrating warm-up and cool-down time into your schedule: Add warm-up and cool-down time to the Year Hours planned earlier. I suggest that you adjust your selected total Year Hours by the amount of time you plan for warm-up and cool-down (usually 15 to 30 minutes each for workouts of intensity higher than Overdistance or Endurance).

2 Step 2: Actual Dates of 4-Week Cycles

Determine the actual date you will begin training with your plan. Then, using a calendar, count off 4-week blocks and list the dates next to each training cycle. (See Sample Worksheet 6.2.)

The year is divided into thirteen 4-week cycles totaling 52 weeks. You may wish to rearrange this format to include seventeen 3-week cycles or ten 5-week cycles, depending on your experience as to what works best for you. In general, 4-week repetitions are the most popular, and perhaps most natural, length for these cycles. If you are planning a program of 26 weeks or less, it is still necessary to use the same format for planning the training cycles as you would if planning for an entire 52 weeks. You'll just need to abbreviate the length of the training stages and carefully select the emphasis of each cycle.

3 Step 3: Training Stage and Emphasis of Each Cycle

Each training cycle must be designated by stage and emphasis in order to clarify the physiological and psychological goals of that cycle. It is especially important to identify actual dates of your racing season(s) in order to designate the appropriate cycles accordingly. Refer to chapter 3 for a detailed explanation of each of the training stages. Also, there may be particular technical aspects of training requiring emphasis at certain times of the year.

4 Step 4: Percentage of Total Year Volume per Cycle

This is the percentage of the total Year Hours (100%) included in each cycle. Determining this value for each cycle is critical to the strength of the overall plan. Planning for one competitive season per year makes this step less complicated than planning for two or more competitive seasons per year. In general, there is about a 5% to 10% increase per month, starting with the Base stage and ending at the end of the Intensity stage. (See Sample Worksheet 6.2.) The Peak stage usually is about a 20% decrease from the previous Intensity cycle. Competition cycles typically contain 5% to 10% less volume than Peaking stage cycles do. This format holds true for plans involving more than one Competition stage per year, though the increases and decreases might be slightly less steep. Refer to Appendix B master plan templates for your sport if you need more ideas on determining the percentage of total yearly volume per cycle.

Planning a program for 26 weeks or less will require the same format as if you were planning for the entire 52 weeks when projecting

SAMPLE WORKSHEET 6.2:
Determination of each 4-week cycle's character

Training plan for the year May 1988–April 1989
Name Rob Sleamaker
1 Year hours to train 385

Cycle	**2** Date	**3** Stage	**3** Emphasis	**4** % Year hours	**5** Periodization %			
					Weeks			
					1	2	3	4
1	5/3-5/30	Base	Aerobic build-up; strength	7	23	26	29	22
2	5/31-6/27	Base	Aerobic build-up; strength	7	23	26	29	22
3	6/28-7/25	Base	Aerobic build-up; strength	7.5	23	26	29	22
4	7/26-8/22	Base	Aerobic build-up; start intervals	8	23	26	29	22
5	8/23-9/19	Base	Hill intervals; strength	8.5	22	27	33	18
6	9/20-10/17	Intensity	Intervals; start speed and pace work	9	22	27	33	18
7	10/18-11/14	Intensity	Sport specificity for 85% of workouts	9.5	22	27	33	18
8	11/15-12/12	Intensity	High-volume; much restoration between workouts	10	22	27	33	18
9	12/13-1/9	Peaking	Anaerobic speeds, training races	8	23	28	32	16
10	1/10-2/6	Racing	Refine technique	7	23	28	32	16
11	2/7-3/5	Racing	Championships on week 4 of cycle	7	23	28	32	16
12	3/6-4/2	Racing	Late season races	6.5	23	28	32	16
13	4/3-4/30	Restoration		5	25	25	25	25

the percentage of total year volume per cycle. This way, you'll be able to utilize the Year Hours figure you determined earlier in the appropriate manner. Otherwise, you'll find that the actual hours you calculate will be inaccurate and not representative of your intentions for the plan.

5 Step 5: Determination of the Periodization per 4-Week Cycle

A gradual increase in training volume per week for the first 3 weeks of the cycle followed by 1 week of decreased volume for the last week of the cycle will positively stress the body and allow recovery and adaptation to the imposed physiological demands, thereby improving the overall conditioning of your body and your confidence. Typically, the Base stage requires gradual increases and decreases within its cycles, whereas the Intensity, Peak, and Race stages require somewhat more drastic increases and decreases within cycles. Chapter 3 offers a more detailed discussion about periodization, and Sample Worksheet 6.2 together with the master plan templates in Appendix B will help you determine the periodization percentages for each week of the cycle.

Worksheet 6.3: The Percentage of Training Components per 4-Week Cycle

In this step you will need to make decisions about which training components you will use for your plan as well as the percentage of each within each training cycle. For simplicity, Worksheet 3 from Appendix A and Sample Worksheet 6.3 use the components from the SERIOUS system, explained in chapter 4. You may wish to change the names of these components to fit your style, or you may end up using only some of these seven components—that's up to you. However, I must emphasize the importance of using common terminology when planning and discussing training. If you use terminology other than that presented with the SERIOUS acronym, be sure to include a description of the intensity and physiological purpose of each training component.

1 Step 1: Stage

Copy the stage for each cycle as determined in Worksheet 6.2.

SAMPLE WORKSHEET 6.3:
Determination of the percentage of training
components per 4-week cycle

Training plan for the year May 1988-April 1989
Name Rob Sleamaker

Cycle	[1] Stage	[2] Percentage of hours	Percentage per 4-week cycle						
			[3] Speed	Endurance	Race/Pace	Interval	Overdistance	Up/Vertical	Strength
1	Base	7	0	10	0	0	70	0	20
2	Base	7	0	10	0	0	70	0	20
3	Base	7.5	0	10	0	0	70	0	20
4	Base	8	0	5	0	5	70	5	15
5	Base	8.5	0	5	0	6	69	8	12
6	Intensity	9	5	5	5	5	60	10	10
7	Intensity	9.5	5	5	5	5	60	10	10
8	Intensity	10	10	5	5	10	55	5	10
9	Peaking	8	15	5	10	10	50	5	5
10	Racing	7	10	5	15	10	50	0	5
11	Racing	7	10	5	15	10	50	0	5
12	Racing	6.5	10	5	15	10	50	0	5
13	Regeneration	5	0	25	0	0	75	0	0

2 Step 2: Percentage of Hours

Copy the percentage of total training volume per cycle as determined in Worksheet 6.2.

3 Step 3: Percentage of Training Component per Cycle

Each training stage will emphasize a gradual increase in some components but decreases in others. Typically, 60% to 70% of a training cycle during the Base stage will be Overdistance, while 15% to 20% may be Strength. The discussion of training stages in chapter 3 will be useful for deciding these percentages. Also, look back at Worksheet 6.1 to review strengths and weaknesses so that these can be incorporated into your plan at this step. Worksheet 6.3 and the master template plans in Appendix B offer guidance as well.

Worksheet 6.4: Training Plan for the Year—Spreadsheet Calculations

Now you can get out Worksheets 6.1, 6.2, and 6.3, along with your calculator and sharp pencil—you're ready to create your training plan! Worksheet 6.4 will help you gain a clear picture of this process.

1 Step 1: Projected Year Hours to Train

Copy this value from Worksheet 6.2. Remember, you can set up your entire plan, then easily decide to train more or fewer hours per year than originally planned. The integrity of your overall plan will stay intact, though the actual volume will change.

2 Step 2: Training Stage

Copy these from Worksheet 6.2.

3 Step 3: Actual Dates of Each Cycle

Copy these from Worksheet 6.2.

4 Step 4: Percentage of Year Hours per Cycle

Copy these from Worksheet 6.2.

5 Step 5: Actual Hours per Cycle

Multiply your projected total year hours from Step 1 by the percentage of year hours per cycle listed in Step 4. Enter these values on Worksheet 6.4.

6 Step 6: Periodization Pattern

Copy this from Worksheet 6.2.

7 Step 7: Actual Hours per Week

Multiply actual hours per cycle calculated in Step 5 by the periodization value in Step 6. For example, if Cycle 1 actual hours are 25 and Week 1 periodization is 23%, then actual hours for Week 1 will be 5.75 hours (.23 × 25 hours).

8 Step 8: Determining Actual Hours of Each Training Component per Week

Multiply actual hours per week calculated in Step 7 by the percentage of training components per 4-week cycle you determined in Worksheet 6.3. For example, taking the value of 5.75 hours for Week 1 from the example in Step 7, multiply 5.75 by 70% (or .70) if you want to train 70% Overdistance in Cycle 1. Therefore, 5.75 × .70 = 4.025 hours of Overdistance in Week 1 of Cycle 1. Be sure to double-check your calculations for each of these entries as you complete this step.

Worksheet 6.5: The Weekly Pattern for Each 4-Week Cycle

Now that you have created the actual yearly plan, calculate to the minute the amount of training for each component in each week of the year. This will create a balanced weekly training pattern that will indicate which training component to work on, which sport activity to use, intensity, and the actual time in minutes for each workout. Worksheet 6.5 allows you to plan one training cycle at a time. Use the calculations from Worksheet 6.4 to create the weekly pattern for each cycle.

In general, it is best to maintain the same weekly pattern for every week of a given cycle. However, you may want to alter this slightly in some cases. For example, during the Competition stage, you may want to race only twice per month. Therefore on 2 of the weeks you will use up the cycle's total time allotment for racing, and the other 2 weeks you will not race. Another variation you may want to try occasionally will be extra-long Overdistance workouts, such as 5-hour bike rides or daylong hikes, during 1 week of the cycle. Therefore, the other OD workouts of the cycle must be changed to accommodate the time taken from the cycle's OD time allotment. You may decide to take 2 or 3 days off one week, depending on schedule, need for rest, illness, and so on. It's a good idea to be prepared to vary from your plan. The worst habit many athletes have is being slaves to their original plans, neglecting to listen to their bodies and their inner voices, therefore becoming overtrained or ill.

Sample weekly patterns for each stage are outlined at the bottom of Worksheet 6.5. Typically, you'll want to follow some basic rules in creating your weekly patterns. See chapter 3 for more details. Here are some ideas you may want to use:

- Plan a long Overdistance day on a Sunday or a Saturday, when you have more training time. This workout can be as much as 50% of the Overdistance time allotment for the week.
- Strength-training sessions should occur every other day or every 3rd day to allow recovery to take place.
- Plan Interval, Up/Vertical, and Race/Pace days with at least 1 day of lower intensity training between these high–intensity days. Another way of thinking about this is to create a pattern that allows 1 or 2 easy days to follow hard days.
- Follow all Interval, Up/Vertical, Race/Pace, and hard Speed workouts with an easy cool-down of 20 to 30 minutes. The next day should include an Overdistance or Endurance/Easy Distance workout. This promotes recovery from the high-intensity workouts.
- Try to maintain the same weekly patterns for several cycles in a row. The body gets used to consistency. This is particularly important during the Peaking and Competition stages, when recovery from stressful racing is essential. For example, during the Competition stage, you may find that planning Intervals on Wednesday, easy Overdistance and Easy Speed on Thursday, and a short Endurance workout on Friday will help you prepare best for a Saturday race. However, you will find that on some weeks,

SAMPLE WORKSHEET 6.4: Training Plan for the Year—Spreadsheet Calculations

Training plan for the year 19 88 – 89   Objective: Cross-Country Ski Racing 10 km – 25 km Distances

Name Rob Sleamaker

Projected year hours to train 385

	1	2	3	4	5
1 Four-week cycle					
2 Training stage	BASE	BASE	BASE	BASE	BASE
Week numbers	1 - 4	5 - 8	9 - 12	13 - 16	17 - 20
3 Actual dates	5/3 - 5/30	5/31 - 6/27	6/28 - 7/25	7/26 - 8/22	8/23 - 9/19
4 % of year hours	7	7	7.5	8	8.5
5 Actual hours/cycle	26.95	26.95	28.88	30.80	32.73

Actual week number	1	2	3	4	5	6	7	8	9	10	11	12	13	14	15	16	17	18	19	20
6 Periodization pattern	23	26	29	22	23	26	29	22	23	26	29	22	23	26	29	22	22	27	33	18
7 Actual hours/week	6.2	7	7.8	5.9	6.2	7	7.8	5.9	6.6	7.5	8.4	6.4	7.1	8	8.9	6.8	7.2	8.8	10.8	5.9
8 Speed	–	–	–	–	–	–	–	–	–	–	–	–	–	–	–	–	–	–	–	–
Endurance	.62	.7	.78	.59	.62	.7	.78	.59	.66	.75	.84	.64	.36	.4	.44	.34	.36	.44	.54	.3
Race/Pace	–	–	–	–	–	–	–	–	–	–	–	–	–	–	–	–	–	–	–	–
Intervals	–	–	–	–	–	–	–	–	–	–	–	–	.36	.4	.44	.34	.43	.53	.65	.35
Overdistance	4.3	4.9	5.5	4.1	4.3	4.9	5.5	4.1	4.6	5.3	5.9	4.5	5	5.6	6.2	4.8	5	6.1	7.5	4.1
Up/Vertical	–	–	–	–	–	–	–	–	–	–	–	–	.36	.4	.44	.34	.58	.7	8.6	.47
Strength	1.24	1.4	1.6	1.2	1.24	1.4	1.6	1.2	1.32	1.5	1.7	1.3	1.1	1.2	1.4	1	.86	1.06	1.3	.71

(cont.)

SAMPLE WORKSHEET 6.4, continued

	Four-week cycle	6				7				8				9			
2	Training stage	INTENSITY				INTENSITY				INTENSITY				PEAK			
	Week numbers	21 - 24				25 - 28				29 - 32				33 - 36			
3	Actual dates	9/20 - 10/17				10/18 - 11/14				11/15 - 12/12				12/13 - 1/9			
4	% of year hours	9				9.5				10				8			
5	Actual hours/cycle	34.65				36.58				38.50				30.80			
6	Actual week number	21	22	23	24	25	26	27	28	29	30	31	32	33	34	35	36
	Periodization pattern	22	27	33	18	22	27	33	18	22	27	33	18	23	28	32	16
7	Actual hours/week	7.6	9.4	11.4	6.2	8	9.9	12.1	6.6	8.5	10.4	12.7	6.9	7.1	8.6	9.9	4.9
8	Speed	.38	.47	.57	.31	.4	.5	.61	.33	.85	1	1.3	.69	1.07	1.3	1.5	.74
	Endurance	.38	.47	.57	.31	.4	.5	.61	.33	.43	.52	.64	.34	.36	.43	.5	.25
	Race/Pace	.38	.47	.57	.31	.4	.5	.61	.33	.43	.52	.64	.34	.71	.86	.99	.49
	Intervals	.38	.47	.57	.31	.4	.5	.61	.33	.85	1.04	1.3	.69	.71	.86	.99	.49
	Overdistance	4.6	5.6	6.8	3.7	4.8	5.9	7.3	4	4.7	5.7	7	3.8	3.6	4.3	5	2.5
	Up/Vertical	.76	.94	1.14	.62	.8	1	1.2	.66	.43	.52	.64	.34	.36	.43	.5	.25
	Strength	.76	.94	1.14	.62	.8	1	1.2	.66	.85	1.04	1.3	.69	.36	.43	.5	.25

SAMPLE WORKSHEET 6.4, continued

	Four-week cycle	10				11				12				13			
1	Four-week cycle	10				11				12				13			
2	Training stage	RACE				RACE				RACE				RESTORATION			
3	Week numbers	37-40				41-44				45-48				49-52			
4	Actual dates	1/10 - 2/6				2/7 - 3/5				3/6 - 4/2				4/3 - 4/30			
5	% of year hours	7				7				6.5				5			
6	Actual hours/cycle	26.95				26.95				25.03				19.25			
7	Actual week number	37	38	39	40	41	42	43	44	45	46	47	48	49	50	51	52
8	Periodization pattern	23	28	32	16	23	28	32	16	23	28	32	16	25	25	25	25
	Actual hours/week	6.2	7.5	8.6	4.3	6.2	7.5	8.6	4.3	5.8	7	8	4	4.8	4.8	4.8	4.8
	Speed	.62	.75	.86	.43	.62	.75	.86	.43	.58	.7	.8	.4	-	-	-	-
	Endurance	.31	.38	.43	.22	.31	.38	.43	.22	.29	.35	.4	.2	1.2	1.2	1.2	1.2
	Race/Pace	.93	1.31	1.3	.65	.93	1.31	1.3	.65	.98	1.05	1.2	.6	-	-	-	-
	Intervals	.62	.75	.86	.43	.62	.75	.86	.43	.58	.7	.8	.4	-	-	-	-
	Overdistance	3.1	3.8	4.3	2.2	3.1	3.8	4.3	2.2	2.9	3.5	4	2	3.6	3.6	3.6	3.6
	Up/Vertical	-	-	-	-	-	-	-	-	-	-	-	-	-	-	-	-
	Strength	.31	.38	.43	.22	.31	.38	.43	.22	.29	.35	.4	.2	-	-	-	-

you'll want to change this pattern slightly to accommodate a very long OD workout or to make things fit in terms of the logistics of your everyday schedule or of the availability of facilities.

1 Step 1: Training Cycle Number

Copy the training cycle number from Worksheet 6.4 to Worksheet 6.5.

2 Step 2: Actual Dates of Training Cycle and of Each Week

Copy the actual dates from Worksheet 6.4 to Worksheet 6.5.

3 Step 3: Objective

This describes the training component for each workout of the cycle's weekly pattern. Refer to the sample at the bottom of Worksheet 6.5.

4 Step 4: Sport

Decide which sport activity you will use for the workout. This does not mean that your decision will be cast in stone. You may want to run one week and ride your mountain bike the next. As a general rule, the closer you come to the Competition stage, the more sport-specific you need to be.

5 Step 5: Intensity

Each workout has a specific physiological purpose, which is monitored by the intensity. In chapter 5, five levels of intensity were described in relation to heart rate and subjective feelings. Also, each SERIOUS training component has been assigned a relative intensity. The actual calculation process for determining correct heart rate intensity ranges for each of the five levels is described in chapter 5. Turn to Table 5.2 (pp. 68-69) now and calculate your heart rate intensity values. Then return to Worksheet 6.5 and enter these values in the appropriate space.

6 Step 6: Time in Minutes per Workout

Refer to Worksheet 6.4 for this step. You've already calculated actual time per week for each training component, and you've chosen a weekly pattern for training with those components. Now you need to decide how much of each component you will use on each day. The sample at the bottom of Worksheet 6.5 identifies the associated percentage of training component time allotment during the week. Generally, you'll find that you'll need to divide Overdistance and Strength time allotments between 2 or 3 days during the week. The other components, because of the relatively small total time for each, will easily be planned into one workout for each.

Adjusting Weekly Patterns

A reminder: It's all right to change the weekly pattern within a cycle. For example, one week you may want to plan Wednesday as your day off because of a dentist appointment, and the next week keep Friday as the planned day off. Or, you may wish to make a daylong OD hike one week that will use up the entire week's OD time allotment. In this case, it would be best to steal some OD time from the other weeks or take off one of the planned OD workouts from the same week.

You'll find, as the year progresses, that weekly patterns will begin to make more sense to you and that a steady routine will work best, both in terms of your body's adaptation and of lifestyle logistics. Make the pattern fit these considerations at the outset, and your training will truly enhance your lifestyle rather than "buck" it all the time.

Remaining Flexible in Your Planning

Training plans can be modified. You are in control of your plan, and it's a good idea to remain in control rather than become a slave to it. The planning you have done in this chapter has allowed you to think carefully about your training. Now you have documentation that outlines what you are planning to do, how often, how much, and at what intensity levels. Every workout is very much related to the others. If you need to make changes in the plan, such as with total Year Hours, then you can make the changes quickly while maintaining the integrity of the entire plan and clearly seeing how the changes affect the overall plan. Gone are the days when your plan consisted of deciding what you were going to do 5 minutes before you ran out the door. Now you have detailed plans that you yourself designed and that you can change at any time. Also, you have recorded these plans so that next year you can reflect on the plans and make necessary changes to strengthen the areas needing improvement and further improve your strongest characteristics.

WORKSHEET 6.5:
Determining the Weekly Pattern for Each 4-Week Cycle

1 Training cycle # 1		**2** Actual dates of cycle 5/3 - 5/30						
				Week # & date				
				1	2	3	4	
Day	**3** Objective	**4** Sport	**5** Intensity	**6** Time (in minutes) per workout				
1A	Overdistance	Ski	I	129	147	165	123	
B	Off							
2A	Endurance	Run	II	12	14	16	11	
B	Strength	Circuit	I	24	28	32	23	
3A	Overdistance	Ski	I	64	74	83	61	
B	Off							
4A	Endurance	Run	II	12	14	16	11	
B	Strength	Weights	I	24	28	32	23	
5A	Overdistance	Cycle	I	64	74	83	61	
B	Off							
6A	Endurance	Aerobics	II	12	14	16	11	
B	Strength	Weights	I	24	28	32	23	
7A	Off							
B	Off							

WORKSHEET 6.5, continued

Typical weekly patterns and associated percentage of training components for base, intensity, peak, and race stages of the training year (based on percent of total time allotment per training component)

Day	Base Objective	%	Intensity Objective	%	Peak Objective	%	Racing Objective	%
1A	OD	50	OD	50	OD	50	OD	50
B	OFF		OFF		OFF		OFF	
2A	EN	33	UP	100	UP	100	OFF	
B	ST	33	ST	50	ST	100	OFF	
3A	OD	25	OD	25	OD	25	OD	25
B	OFF		OFF		SP	50	SP	50
4A	EN	33	IN	100	IN	100	IN	100
B	ST	33	ST	50	OFF		OFF	
5A	OD	25	OD	25	OD	25	OD	25
B	OFF		SP	100	SP	100	SP	100
6A	EN	33	EN	100	EN	100	EN	100
B	ST	33	OFF		OFF		OFF	
7A	OFF		RP	100	RP	100	RP	100
B	OFF		OFF		OFF		OFF	

SP = Speed
EN = Endurance
RP = Race/Pace
IN = Intervals

OD = Overdistance
UP = Up/Vertical
ST = Strength

THE SERIOUS SYSTEM TRAINING LOG AND JOURNAL

Why record training information, especially after so carefully planning your training? Investing in that careful planning involves the expense of your precious time, energy, and money—which is precisely the reason for keeping a training log. A well-kept log of essential information is the best means for evaluating your progress over the long haul. Without a well-kept record of training, it becomes very difficult to objectively view high points and low points in training and to track trends and idiosyncrasies in your training.

In this chapter, you will learn about

- the benefits of keeping a training log and journal;
- the essential components of a good log;
- the SERIOUS System log and journal;
- ways to monitor stress during training and skills to make adjustments to the training plan, based on stress signals; and
- methods for detecting trends and tracking progress in training.

Benefits of Maintaining an Effective Training Log

I've been fortunate to have worked with many top endurance athletes over the years. One observation I've made is that the best usually keep detailed logs and journals and are able to mine gems of information from their logs. A couple of stories illustrates this well.

Two years ago, one of the skiers I know was having terrible results in preseason races and training. She skied the World Championship team tryouts but failed to make the team and became extremely sick afterward. Her performance was unusually poor, because she had been expected to end up at the top of the pile. Depressed and confused by her mysterious drop in performance, she came to me for my ear and my advice. After listening to her story of the events leading up to the racing season, I began to put a few pieces of the puzzle together. Still, I needed hard data on training hours, what those hours consisted of, recovery information, and general comments from journal entries. She presented a fairly thorough training log upon request.

I pored over the log, searching for clues. Every time I came to a place where I found a clue, I recorded it. When I was finished, we reviewed my clue list. In June she had undergone arthroscopic knee surgery. Although she had been given some guidelines for rehabilitation, it was apparent that she had stressed the knee too much too soon, because for the next 4 months of journal entries, her comments about the knee indicated weakness of the joint and her own fears of reinjury during training. In July she had seen a new coach who placed her on a different training plan. He did not realize the extent of her injury and started her on too much volume for her current fitness level.

In October her relationship with her boyfriend ended. In November she experienced a financial crunch where she put herself under a lot of stress working to meet some deadlines. Also, she went to West Yellowstone, Montana, to get on the early snow. The reaction of most skiers to early snow is to be so elated that they ski their brains out for 5 days and are then exhausted. I call it the "crash and burn" approach—rather self-destructive in nature. Our skier was no exception. She couldn't resist the temptation of getting out there with her teammates and skiing all day long.

Her log entries during November and December were revealing. I boiled them down and found a distinct pattern in her training. She would feel good and ski hard for 3 days. During the 3rd day she would "bonk," becoming exhausted even on short sessions. On the 4th and 5th days, she would rest and recover. The 6th day would be a race or timed trial, and because she always felt better by race time, she'd go out there and hammer (in the early part of the season, no less!). The 7th day would mean a nosedive for the bed.

As she started each new 7-day cycle, she would be slightly more worn down than a week before. When the tryout series finally arrived in January, she was a wreck. Her immune system was weak. She contracted influenza almost immediately after arriving at the Olympic Training Center in Lake Placid, a haven for viral infections because so many athletes from around the world are constantly coming and going. She bonked at the midway point of each of the 4 races of the series. No medals, no trip to Europe, no fun.

Our critical review taught us both a lot. The best prescription for her was to take 2 to 3 weeks of total rest—no training, no stress. She followed this prescription and was able to come back and ski quite well later that season. Most importantly, some valuable lessons had been learned. If she had not kept the log and journal, it would have been extremely difficult piecing together her training history with any accuracy.

The second story, mentioned briefly at the beginning of chapter 1, is about Sigvart Bjontegaard, head coach of the U.S. Olympic biathlon team from 1986 to 1988 and a former national champion biathlete in Norway. One day when we were discussing training, he pulled out 12 neatly kept training diaries. They were the logs he had used during his 12 years of training with the national team in Norway. Recorded for each week, month, and year were volume of training, what that volume of training consisted of, recovery data, subjective feelings, and so on. At the end of each booklet was a foldout graph with the 52 weeks on the horizontal axis and the percentage of weekly hours on the vertical axis. The completed chart was multicolored and detailed. He had used a bar graph to color code the percentage of each week's hourly volume by training component, such as OD, Speed, Strength, Interval, and so on (see Figure 7.1).

He laid all these yearly graphs next to each other and proceeded to describe which years were his most successful. We analyzed his most successful years and discovered some very interesting patterns. These seemed to agree with much of the scientific and coaching literature available today. He had inadvertently become a scientist, a data collector—a keen, objective observer of his own training progress. Now he could use that data to help the athletes he was coaching.

There are countless other stories about using training logs to objectify and enhance training. The point is that without a good system for logging training data, the likelihood of becoming lost in a sea of observations, feelings, advice from others, and your own personal information is much greater. A systematic approach to collecting information about training is essential for staying on track and for making significant gains in understanding the training plans and methods that work best for you.

Using the Log/Journal System

The SERIOUS training log/journal system has been developed to match the record-keeping needs for using the SERIOUS training components,

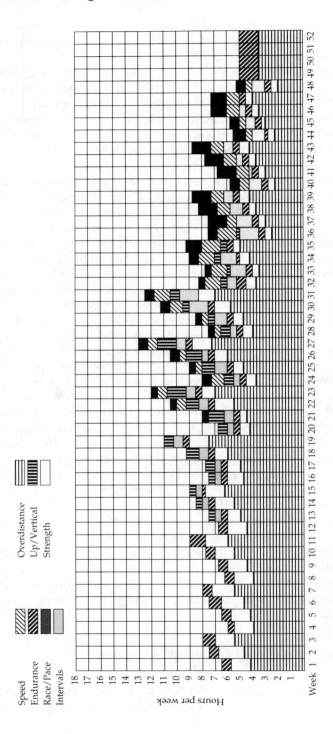

Figure 7.1 A yearlong performance graph can provide an objective and valuable assessment of your strengths and of areas needing improvement.

but it can be modified to work well with any systematic training plan and associated training components. It is designed to enable you to track progress, detect trends, balance training, and monitor stress and overtraining with ease and without spending a lot of time recording tedious details. Refer to Appendix D for blank versions of the SERIOUS system log, journal, and yearlong performance graph.

The Log

Figure 7.2 illustrates the design of this log and is completed to serve as a model for using it correctly. The following is a description of the components of the log and how to complete it:

1. Week #: This is the week number of the year plan in which you are presently training.
2. Day/Date: It is important to maintain a consistent weekly pattern for accomplishing workouts from your plan.
3. Training Time of SERIOUS Components: Record time in minutes for each component worked on in a given day. These will be totaled at the end of each week.
4. Intensity: Mark the intensity either as the actual heart rate value or with a number I through V, V being the most intense level, for each workout. Check your training plan to be certain you completed the workout at the prescribed intensity.
5. Training Activity: Mark the activity you used for each workout. If you use more than one activity to complete the session, such as running and cycling, note the minutes of training for each in the space provided. You'll want to go over your log at the end of the year and figure the amount of time you trained in each activity.
6. Stretching: Record minutes of stretching. From 15 to 30 minutes per day is best. You may want to note the routine you used in the journal section (Figure 7.3).
7. Feeling: This is based on a scale of 1 to 5, with 1 being the absolute worst feeling and 5 being a fantastic race or training session. Basically, it represents your mental set for the training session. Too many entries of 1s may indicate that you are overtraining. Likewise, many entries of 5s could mean that you are about to peak (hopefully not too early!).
8. Workout completed: Mark with a ''NO'' if you fail to complete the last scheduled workout due to fatigue during the session. Failing to complete a planned workout may be a sign of stress. If you do not complete a planned workout because of a scheduling conflict or another nonphysical reason, there is no need for alarm.

Week #___	Day Time	1 A	1 B	2 A	2 B	3 A	3 B	4 A	4 B	5 A	5 B	6 A	6 B	7 A	7 B	Totals
Date		6	14	6	15	6	16	6	17	6	18	6	19	6	20	
Speed																
Endurance					25			20			80	30				
Race/Pace																
Interval									25							
Overdistance		90	120				74									
Up/Vertical													40			
Strength				30				30				30				
Intensity (I - V)		I	I	I	II		I	II	IV		II	II	IV			
Bicycle											MTN Bike					
Hiking																
Rowing																
Ski X-C		Roller Ski				Roller Ski										
Swimming																
Running					✓			✓	✓			✓	✓			
Other			Ca-noe	ST 1				ST 1				ST 2				
Stretching		15		15				15	15			15	15			
Feeling (1 - 5)		4	4	3	3		3.5	3	3		1	2	1			
Workout completed? Y/N		Y	Y	Y	Y			Y	Y		Y	Y	N	N		
Morning pulse		42		41		44		45		52		54		48		
Morning weight		152		151		152		149		149		150		150		
Sleep hours		7		8		6.5		6		6		9		8		

(Vertical notations in the Day 7 columns: "RETIRED" and "OFF")

Figure 7.2 A SERIOUS system training log completed correctly. Note the stress monitor signs highlighted, indicating overstress.

9. Morning Pulse: An increase in your morning pulse, taken before rising, of more than 10% over normal usually means stress or overtraining. Training, family, relationships, work, or financial problems may affect this. Your body is telling you to rest. You'll

need to adjust your plan. (NOTE: you may need to void before taking a.m. pulse, because a full bladder can sometimes cause an elevated heart rate.)

10. Morning Weight: Weigh yourself consistently at the same time in the morning under the same conditions, before breakfast but after voiding. Losses of more than 3% body weight usually represent fluid loss. If so, take an easy day of training and replenish fluids. A loss of body weight in water of more than 5% is dangerous and could lead to overheating or even heatstroke.

11. Sleep: Record hours of sleep. Ten percent less than normal is a signal to take an easy day and catch up on rest.

The Journal

It is a good idea to record thoughts, feelings, life situations, or other observations in journal form. A journal is also a good place to record distances covered in training, weather conditions, training partners, and equipment used that day. If you do not like to write, this may not be for you; in this case, keep very accurate log records. However, a great deal of vitally important information can be gained by looking back through a well-kept journal. Journal entries should correspond with log entry dates. Figure 7.3 illustrates the SERIOUS system journal.

Stress Signals

You can monitor overtraining and stress as well as your progress by evaluating your recordings for a.m. pulse, a.m. weight, sleep hours, and incompletion of workouts. If any one of these is abnormal according to the descriptions that follow, you should take it as a sign to prepare to alter the day's training. Consider it a red flag of warning. If any two of these are abnormal, consider these as two red flags of warning and *definitely* adjust your training for the day, either by reducing the time, changing the intensity, or taking the day off and getting more rest.

These stress monitors are only predictors. Use common sense and listen to your body for the answers. Also, depending on your situation, you may have to make adjustments for outside stressors you have very little control over. Travel (especially changing time zones during air travel), altitude, humidity, heat, extreme cold, long work hours, family schedules, and other factors can affect the quality of your recovery from training. Recovery and restoration from training and other stressors will be discussed in greater detail in chapter 10.

Balance and Trends in Training

Keeping a detailed log is not difficult and will provide you with the data you—and perhaps coaches, doctors, or sports scientists—will need to evaluate your training objectively. Perhaps the most important concept behind logging is that of balance. Balance between overtraining and undertraining will require continuously checking your state of training—revealed in your log. In order to maintain the fine balance required for optimizing your potential and minimizing any downtime, disciplined logging is essential. The SERIOUS training log system is logical and easy to follow. All you need is the commitment to make it work for you.

As I mentioned earlier, you can use a well-kept log to identify trends in performance, stress, and other important information. Perhaps one of the most valuable discoveries you can make is a trend that led up to a training day or race that you subjectively felt and recorded as a 5. Study the weeks before the day you rated so highly. You may be able to connect key factors to that banner performance.

Conversely, you may also be able to identify negative trends. Perhaps you really don't like training with Joe Cool because every time you do, he pushes you to go harder and faster than you have planned on your schedule. Eliminate the stress—either work out a compromise or refrain from training with Joe. Or, you may notice that you are having pains in your left knee after about 300 miles on those new shoes. Maybe it's time for a new pair. The list goes on and on. Have fun discovering these trends for yourself.

Journal

Day/Date		Week of 1 / 2 / 89 Week # 1
2	1	Slept really well; a little congested still. Hiked 15 miles with JBL to Gothic and back; tired at end, but felt comfortable entire hike. A little low on fluids at night.
3	2	Congested and a little sore in the a.m. Otherwise good rest.
4	3	Ran with Janet — race trail. p.m. run with poles — race trail and around golf course. Felt very good.
5	4	Roller ski at Range. 6 x 12 min. intervals. Used T-poles and got better w/time. Raced Biathlon foot race. 3 x 2:30 intervals. Shot 5/10 3p 2s hits Overall good day.
6	5	South Rd. roller ski; a bit tired. Used super G's, 40 min.; T-poles, 40 min. Tired at end but good.
7	6	Day off
8	7	Canoed 2 hrs. at lake — easy. Slept alot during the day!

Figure 7.3 A well-kept training log and journal is a key to successful training.

WARMING UP, STRETCHING, AND COOLING DOWN

Many of us learned that warm-up was synonymous with stretching. Fifteen minutes of jumping jacks, bouncing, toe touches, and various other contortions was considered enough preparation for a vigorous workout. However, these are no longer considered safe and proper forms of warm-up.

In this chapter, you will learn about

- the benefits of warm-up,
- the physiological basis for proper warm-up,
- how to warm up properly before training and competition,
- the benefits of stretching for improved flexibility,
- basic guidelines for stretching properly, and
- how cool-down exercise helps speed recovery.

All of these are worth serious consideration by every endurance athlete.

Warm-Up

The aim of a proper warm-up routine is to achieve better results in the training or performance following it. Warming up refers to the raising of body temperature or, more specifically, muscle temperature through active or passive means. Active warm-up is aerobic muscular work during which metabolism increases. The metabolic processes of the muscle cells are temperature dependent, with increases in metabolism noted at higher temperatures. Astrand and Rodahl (1977) indicate that the metabolic rate of the cell increases by 13% for every degree of temperature increase in the muscle. The exchange of oxygen from the blood to the tissues is increased at higher intramuscular temperatures. Asmussen and Boje (1960) discovered that physical work capacity is increased following proper warm-up.

Passive warm-up involves the use of external means to elevate body temperature, such as saunas, hot showers, whirlpool baths, heating pads, and massage. DeVries (1959) showed that although passive warm-up has been shown to improve performance times, active warm-up has resulted in even better performances. Thus, this discussion will focus on active warm-up methods.

Injury prevention is another important reason for including proper warm-up before vigorous training. Increases in muscle temperature increase the elasticity of muscle tissue, reducing the risks of strains or tears. Also, it appears that gradual warm-up preceding vigorous activity is important in prevention of cardiac injuries. Barnard (1973) reported that warming up properly can prevent certain electrocardiographic abnormalities that are sometimes seen in seemingly healthy persons at the beginning of intense running performances. Athletes over 35, especially those with a family history of heart disease, are advised to consider this evidence.

Proper Warm-Up Prior to Training Sessions

Preceding all Speed, Race/Pace, Interval, Up/Vertical, and Strength training sessions (Overdistance and Endurance being exceptions because they are performed at low intensity), you should incorporate 10 to 30 minutes of moderate-intensity (Level II heart rate) aerobic activity using the planned training activity. It is best that the warm-up end no more than 10 minutes before you begin the training session. This is particularly important prior to the start of a race or timed trial. A longer lag time will result in a cooling of tissue and a reversion of metabolic processes toward resting states.

Proper Warm-Up Prior to Competitions

Karvonen (1978) studied the physiological effects of warm-up in cross-country skiers and cross-country runners, showing conclusively that proper warm-up improved performance for these athletes. He tested athletes with and without warm-up routines in various competitions and measured objective data, such as performance times, rectal temperature, heart rate, and venous blood lactic acid concentration, and registered the athletes' subjective performance evaluations. The results showed that not only did the athletes subjectively feel that competition was easier following warm-ups, but race results were significantly better for athletes who warmed up.

The warm-up routine in Karvonen's research involved general warming up of 10 to 20 minutes for cross-country skiers and 20 to 40 minutes for runners. The warm-up intensity was medium, with some higher intensity, faster tempo bursts incorporated in the middle of the warm-up period. Hogberg and Ljunggren (1947) showed that a warm-up of 15 to 30 minutes at a relatively high rate of energy expenditure just prior to competition improved overall performance.

It seems that the intensity and duration of the warm-up must also be adjusted for environmental conditions. Robinson (1963) observed that warming up in the heat (90 degrees F) caused rectal temperatures of road runners to be 1.5 degrees higher than those who did not warm up prior to a 10K race. The increase in rectal temperature prior to racing in the heat may be a detriment to performance due to implications associated with overheating.

Improved Flexibility Through Stretching

Stretching is not synonymous with warming up. Generally, I do not recommend stretching as part of the warm-up routine. The likelihood of injury may increase if stretching is initiated before the muscles are properly warmed up. However, stretching does have a place in endurance sports training. Where, when, and how you incorporate stretching into your program are the keys (Figure 8.1).

Benefits of Stretching

Intense physical training generally strengthens the specific muscle groups associated with the training activity. However, these muscle groups and the connective tissue surrounding them usually become less flexible as they strengthen. The decrease in flexibility is accompanied by an increase in the probability of injury due to increased muscle fiber and connective tissue tension, as well as a decreased range

Figure 8.1 Stretching exercises are most effective after a complete warm-up or following a workout.

of motion, which inhibits proper technique. All athletes need to be concerned with injury prevention, and achieving greater range of motion may help improve performance. Examples of improved performance include longer strides in running, greater pull stroke in swimming, improved ability to ride a flat ski in cross-country skiing, and becoming more aerodynamic in cycling.

Stretching Before Vigorous Training

If you plan to stretch before vigorous training, especially prior to speed or strength sessions that require substantial range of motion, always warm up first according to the guidelines presented previously. Use the following guidelines for stretching properly:

1. Use mild static stretches of every muscle group that will be used during training. Move into a stretching position and hold each

stretch at the point of comfortable tension, NEVER to the point of pain.
2. Hold each static stretch for 15 to 60 seconds. Avoid ballistic, or bouncing-type, stretches, which increase the likelihood of over-stretching and straining the muscles and connective tissue.
3. Inhale through your nose before each stretch, and exhale through the mouth as you begin the stretch.
4. Once in a stretching position, make an inventory of your body's condition, relaxing those muscles not involved in the primary stretch, then refocusing on the muscles you are trying to stretch.

Post-exercise Stretching

This is the optimal time for stretching because the muscles are warmed up. Follow these steps:

1. Cool down with low-level activity for 10 to 15 minutes following any hard exercise. Change into dry clothing and put on a warm-up suit or wind suit (and a dry hat in cold weather).
2. Find a warm, dry place to stretch. Some relaxing music may be helpful.
3. Following the guidelines for pre-exercise stretching, concentrate on those muscle groups used hardest in training. This is a good time to stretch all other areas, too.
4. You may want to jostle and massage the major muscle groups a bit before you stretch them. This can help relax them.

General Guidelines for Flexibility Exercises

- Stretch regularly, every day if possible. Gymnasts and aerobics instructors become so flexible only by spending hours each day stretching. I know of one instructor who claims that she often watches TV or reads the newspaper while in a split and with her elbows on the floor in front of her.
- Use slow, static stretches. Do not bounce. Instead, relax the muscles and ease into the stretch, stopping before you feel pain or much tension. Breathe in and out regularly, releasing any tension you may be feeling. Hold each stretch for 15 to 60 seconds, increasing the stretch gradually.

- Set realistic goals for stretching. There is no need for you to "out-stretch" anyone or to improve much over the previous day. Just release the muscular tension in a comfortable way, and your flexibility will gradually improve.
- Increases in flexibility will be greater if stretching is performed after activity when the muscle temperature is high.

You'll have to discover a formula that works well for you. I find that stretching works best if I do it in the middle or at the end of the day, after I have been active. Often, I will sit in a sauna or hot tub and stretch my tight hamstrings with great success. It is important to consider flexibility training as something that will give you long-term benefits rather than as a specific warm-up or injury prevention exercise prior to intense training. With proper warm-up, the muscles will naturally be ready for intense movement.

Anderson (1980) has provided a good reference for learning flexibility exercises and techniques. Also, qualified aerobics, gymnastics, and dance instructors, as well as athletic trainers and physical therapists, can show you proper stretching techniques.

Cool-Down

Intense exercise is usually accompanied by a buildup of metabolic waste, such as lactic acid, and often may cause slight tears or ruptures in the connective tissue. Both conditions can lead to soreness. In particular, it is necessary to remove metabolic waste to enhance recovery from training. A warm-down period following exercise has been shown to markedly speed removal of lactic acid.

Shevciw (1986) reported a study of the German National Junior Hockey Team, the members of which performed a 3000-meter run that brought them to a condition of high lactic acid buildup. Immediately after the run, a 20-milliliter sample of blood was taken from each athlete. Three additional blood samples were drawn at 3 minutes, 6 minutes, and 30 minutes after the run. Between the 6-minute and the 30-minute blood samples, half of the athletes ran a 15-minute cool-down run at subthreshold intensity, while the other half of the group rested. The blood samples taken at 30 minutes post-run showed that the athletes who used the cool-down run had significantly lower levels of lactic acid than athletes who rested.

I have observed several top athletes consistently using a cool-down after all hard training and racing. At the 1987 World Biathlon Championships, I watched American Josh Thompson win the silver medal in the 20K race—the first medal ever won by an American male in

World Cup biathlon competition. After brief celebration with coaches and teammates, he changed into a dry warm-up suit and skied a 30-minute cool-down before facing the deluge of fans and reporters!

Ideally, the cool-down should be performed in the same manner as the warm-up. Fifteen to 30 minutes of Level I exercise, using the same activity you used for training that day, will be about right. Fifteen to 30 minutes of easy aerobic activity should follow strength work-outs. There's no need to cool-down after OD or Endurance training because they are accomplished at cool-down intensity anyway. It's a good idea to change into dry clothing (and a dry hat if it's cold) before you start the cool-down. This will prevent you from getting chilled. It's also a good idea to begin drinking fluids during your cool-down. After you've cooled down enough, find a warm, dry place to start your stretching routine.

NUTRITION FOR OPTIMAL PERFORMANCE

I n endurance sports the major limiting factor from a nutritional perspective is chronically inadequate carbohydrate intake. Gollnick (1985) determined that carbohydrates (CHO) provide the primary fuel during intense muscular endurance activity. Therefore, high CHO consumption by endurance athletes on a daily basis is recommended and is the focus of this chapter. Systematic training provides us with an overall perspective regarding energy expenditure and the respective energy requirements for different types, durations, and intensities of daily exercise. The following topics will be discussed in this chapter:

- Overview of the energy nutrients: carbohydrates, proteins, and fats
- Benefits of the high-carbohydrate diet
- The carbo factor: how to get the right stuff(ing)
- Pre- and post-race diets
- The fluid factor: water, the essential nutrient

Overview of the Energy Nutrients

Food is fuel for your high-performance engine—your body. That's how I like to look at sports nutrition. The analogy works because the best fuel for sport performance also seems to be the best for health maintenance and disease prevention. It's essential that you learn about the foods that will supply you with the right fuel (Figure 9.1).

High-performance nutrition involves a definitive combination of carbohydrates, fat, protein, vitamins, minerals, and water. The mixture should be approximately the same for most endurance athletes. However, it is helpful to understand the definition and function of each of these nutrients as they relate to optimal performance and good health.

Figure 9.1 Wholesome foods are essential to successful training.

Carbohydrates: The Predominant Energy Nutrient

Carbohydrates and fats are the predominant fuel nutrients. The body prefers to use these first as energy sources. Carbohydrates are found in a number of foods including table sugar, whole grains, starches, vegetables, and fruits. Once digested, these foods are used for energy in basically the same way. Processed carbohydrates are found mobile in the bloodstream as glucose or are stored in the muscles and liver as glycogen. Excess supply is converted to free fatty acids and stored as adipose tissue (body fat).

Dietary fat (found in meats, dairy products, poultry, fish, oils, and nuts) is also an important energy source. It is used as fuel in combination with carbohydrates. Fat is stored in the body as adipose tissue when excess fat, carbohydrates, or protein is ingested. This stored fat is the body's largest energy reservoir, although not necessarily its most efficiently utilized source.

According to Holloszy and Booth (1976), the body will burn carbohydrates as the major source of energy during intense (over 65% $\dot{V}O_2$max) endurance exercise. It is the fuel most readily available to the muscle cells. The only problem is that we can store only a limited amount of carbohydrates in the body. Scientists estimate that the average 150-pound, well-trained, male endurance athlete can store some 1,800 kilocalories as glycogen and glucose. A well trained female endurance athlete weighing 120 pounds can store about 1,550 kilocalories.

This energy reserve translates into about 90 to 180 minutes of continuous exercise, depending on the athlete's efficiency, intensity, and environmental considerations. Heavy training and competition will deplete these glycogen stores in about 2 hours. You may be familiar with the marathoner's dilemma of "hitting the wall." This describes the condition of depleting the body's glycogen stores during training or races. The condition is characterized by feelings of severe fatigue, dizziness, local muscle pains, and abnormally elevated heart rate. The body is able to continue exercise, but at a much-reduced intensity or rate because now the body's fat stores must almost single-handedly meet the energy requirements. Burning fat alone is a very inefficient way to fuel exercise. The best way to prevent this situation is to raise the pre-exercise muscle glycogen content to the highest possible levels.

It is important to remember the fact that your glycogen storage capacity can be increased through proper training and diet. If you train so as to deplete the glycogen in the tissue and then eat a proper carbohydrate-fat-protein mix, the muscle cells will gain the capability to store slightly more glycogen than they did before. Of course, there are limits to this glycogen storage—usually about 1,800 to 2,000 kilocalories for highly trained endurance athletes. However, systematic training can, by stimulating your body to adapt to increasing demands, improve glycogen storage capacity (assuming that CHO is made available in the diet). This is a gradual, long-term process; you can't just load up on carbohydrates and go out and expect to do well in a triathlon.

How much of your diet needs to be carbohydrates? Most sport nutrition research indicates that at least 55% to 65% of the diet should consist of carbohydrates (primarily complex). This applies to everyone, athletes and nonathletes alike. Endurance athletes may need to get more than 70% of their energy from carbohydrates, depending upon how much time is spent training and the intensity of that training.

Unfortunately, the typical American diet contains less than 50% carbohydrates. Powerful economic and social influences have conditioned the American consumer to purchase large amounts of meat and dairy products, both of which are high in fat and protein while relatively low in carbohydrates. Athletes subject to such eating habits often fail to adequately replenish glycogen stores on a day-to-day basis. Chronic glycogen depletion (even several consecutive days' worth) can result in overtraining, injuries, and subpar performances.

A recent experience illustrates this point well. An elite runner came to see me for advice regarding his apparently downward-spiraling performances. He described chronic fatigue and lethargy during training and in recovery. His last four races had been terrible, and in one 15K race, he began to black out as he ran the last few kilometers. Otherwise, mentally he was still sharp, with work productivity and family life going well. Yet he couldn't figure out the reason for his pitiful performances.

I started asking questions. I immediately ruled out hypohydration because he was doing well with fluid replacement. Then I looked at his training log. Two weeks before racing season, he had been sick with the flu. When he recovered, he jumped right back into his high-intensity training stage in order to peak for the first big races. Speed work, Intervals, and Pace work made up the bulk of his training—all of these burn carbohydrates.

Beginning to piece the puzzle together, I analyzed his diet by having him keep accurate records of everything he consumed for a week. The analysis depicted that which I had suspected all along—chronic glycogen depletion due to inadequate replenishment. He was consuming a diet that was 40% carbohydrate, 17% protein, and a whopping 43% fat. As soon as he had resumed training after his illness, he dove headlong into this chronic state. No wonder he was bonking in races!

I quickly gave him a crash course in sport nutrition and provided him with a diet plan that included 70% carbohydrates. We worked hard to improve his nutritional awareness and his skills for identifying foods that would give him the right amount of carbohydrates and eliminate the high-fat foods from his diet. Within a few weeks, he was back to racing and training at his potential.

Ellsworth, Hewitt, and Haskell (1985) identified similar circumstances in elite cross-country skiers. The point is that many athletes may believe they are consuming adequate amounts of carbohydrates, whereas analyses of their intake would reveal otherwise.

Fats in the Diet: How Much Is Necessary?

Very little. At most, 25% of your calories should be from fat sources. Most Americans consume 40% to 45% of their diet from fatty foods.

Not only are they failing to replace precious glycogen in sufficient quantity to meet heavy training demands, but they may be subject to the many illnesses related to high-fat diets. The risk of having excessive blood cholesterol, heart disease, high blood pressure, diverticulosis, cancer, obesity, and other diseases increases with high-fat diets.

Fats are generally either overt or "hidden." Overt fats are foods such as oils, butter, margarine, lard, and visible fat on meats. Hidden fats are found in combination with other foods—fried foods, baked goods made with lots of oil or butter, fatty meats, whole-milk dairy products, eggs, nuts, and nut butters. It's often difficult to recognize fats in the diet, but they sure add up. If you eat any of the foods just listed on a regular basis, especially meats and dairy products, without attention to their fat content, you're probably eating too much fat.

Some fat in the diet is necessary. It is used for insulating nerves, in the manufacture of certain hormones, and for cell membranes. It is an important energy source, too.

"Fat is burned in the flame of carbohydrates" is an expression used to describe the energy utilization mechanism of the muscle cells. At low- to moderate-intensity exercise, there can be a glycogen-sparing effect if fat can contribute to the energy supplied to the muscle. However, note that abundant fat is stored in adipose tissue even in the trimmest of athletes. This fat can be used for energy. Therefore, most sport nutritionists feel that there is no need to plan diets especially to fulfill a fat intake requirement. Rather, they are concerned with too much fat in the diet. Josh Thompson, one of the top biathletes and cross-country skiers in the world, refers to himself as a "fat-o-phobe"—one who very carefully screens every scrap of food he puts into his mouth to make sure he's not consuming a high-fat item. It is a good idea for all endurance athletes as well as the general population to adopt a bit of "fat-o-phobia" as well.

My recommendation is that very little of the fats you consume should come from animal products. These include red meats, poultry, dairy products (skim-milk products are acceptable), eggs, and animal-fat-based shortenings or margarines. The reason for this is that cholesterols and most saturated fats are present in animal fats only. High-cholesterol, high-fat diets contribute to heart disease and other ailments, and there is no requirement for dietary cholesterol, because the body manufactures its own. Try to change your diet to include the lowest cholesterol and fat levels possible.

Protein: Enough Is Enough!

Are you one of the millions who were brought up on a training table heaped with steak and eggs? The image of Sylvester Stallone as Rocky Balboa downing 3 raw eggs before his morning run still sends a chill down my spine. After all, if muscles are made of protein, isn't it logical that a high-protein diet will help build muscles?

Sounds good, but it isn't true. Of course, muscle *is* in constant need of repair and rebuilding, especially in athletes training hard, and protein for these functions, in the form of essential amino acids found in certain foods, must be present in the diet. However, most Americans consume 50% to 100% more protein than their bodies need for the rebuilding functions. The excess protein they eat will only be excreted in the form of urea. This causes our organs, particularly the kidneys, to work overtime metabolizing the extra protein. In addition, any excess kilocalories from the protein may simply be stored as fat. Thus, eating too much protein wears out our precious organs and adds to unwanted fat.

Animal products do have the virtue of being complete proteins— they contain all the essential amino acids in one package. However, they also contain cholesterol and increased amounts of saturated fats. Used in moderation and with discretion, animal sources of essential amino acids (muscle-cell building blocks) can be an appropriate part of the endurance athlete's diet.

If you don't want to worry about having to get the essential amino acids from a combination of several nonanimal sources, make an effort to choose the leanest of meats. Trim any visible fat away, remove the skins from poultry, discard the egg yolks, and buy only low-fat or skim milk, yogurt, and cheeses. These foods will then have a much-reduced fat and cholesterol content, and the protein will be of high quality. The key is that you don't need to eat a very large serving of any of these in a day. The amount depends on your body weight and training requirements. When in training, you need about 1 to 1.4 grams of complete protein per kilogram of body weight daily.

There are many alternatives to eating animal products as the sole source of dietary protein. Vegetables, legumes, and whole grains in appropriate combinations with each other will provide adequate quantities of essential amino acids. Whole grains such as oats, barley, wheat, and millet contain all of the 44 known essential nutrients (except vitamins B_{12}, C, and D). Grains usually have protein contents ranging between 8% and 15% protein by weight, compared to 30% for beef. However, grains typically contain low levels of the essential amino acids tryptophan and lysine. The wary consumer can remedy this by combining dried beans with the grain dish or by adding a small amount of low-fat animal protein to the meal. Several excellent references listed at the end of this book can help you determine appropriate sources and combinations of proteins.

The extent to which you can utilize fewer animal and more vegetable sources of protein is exemplified by marathon runner Jim Miller, who has developed his own "dinner of champions." We affectionately refer to Jim's evening cuisine as "The Miller Compound," and, believe me, his compound sticks to your ribs! Jim starts with a base of brown rice and lentils cooking in water. As the rice grains become tender, he adds some herb seasonings, vegetables, a can of tuna packed in water, and occasionally some vegetable soup stock. I've witnessed the creation of The Miller Compound on numerous occasions and have seen many variations on the basic recipe; he's even been known to throw in a dab of peanut butter, some low-fat cottage cheese, and raisins. He gets a diet that is very high in complex carbohydrates (about 70%) and that meets enough of his daily protein requirements through the tuna and the combination of the rice and lentils, yet has very little fat.

Benefits of the High-Carbohydrate Diet

There are several reasons for recommending a high-carbohydrate diet. First, it provides the body with the most available energy for training and competition. Next, a high-CHO diet may speed up the recovery process. Finally, it seems that a high-CHO diet can promote good health.

Fuel for Training and Racing

It is estimated that during long-duration exercise sessions, your body will become depleted of its glycogen stores after about 2 hours. Daily maintenance of this glycogen is accomplished by consuming a diet high in CHO. Bergstrom, Hermansen, Hultman, and Saltin (1967) found that endurance (time to exhaustion) is significantly improved when a high-CHO diet is consumed, as illustrated in Figure 9.2.

Restoration

Restoration does not simply refer to what is typically regarded as recovery—such as how you feel after a bit of rest. Rather, it refers more specifically to the process of restoring the muscles and physiological processes that have been stressed during a specific training session. Training at all yearly volumes, particularly those exceeding 350 hours, will produce best results if proper restorative measures are implemented. Diet is an integral part of the restoration plan. Costill and Miller (1980) determined that failure to replenish glycogen daily will likely result in chronic depletion and fatigue, as illustrated in Figure 9.3.

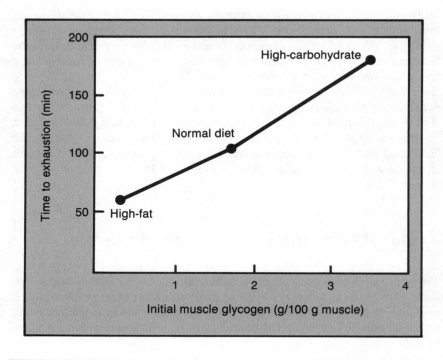

Figure 9.2   Effects of various diets on time to exhaustion in endurance athletes. *Note.* From "Diet, Muscle Glycogen and Physical Performance" by J. Bergstrom, L. Hermansen, E. Hultman, et al., 1967, *Acta Physiologica Scandinavica,* **71**, p. 140. Copyright 1967. Reprinted by permission.

It is recommended that daily carbohydrate consumption remain between 65% and 80% of an endurance athlete's daily caloric intake in order to adequately replenish spent glycogen stores in muscle and liver tissue. While this is ideal, it may not prove to be easy. One study conducted with elite cross-country skiers by Ellsworth, Hewitt, and Haskill (1985) concluded that typical carbohydrate consumption averaged between 39% and 52% of total calorie intake, far below optimal levels.

General Health Maintenance

In most cases an optimal-performance diet high in CHO will also be a healthful, nutritious one. The athlete following a performance-enhancing, high-CHO diet will likely consume copious quantities of

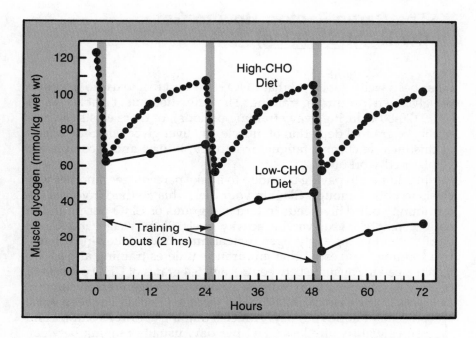

Figure 9.3 High-carbohydrate diet speeds recovery from training. *Note.* From ''Nutrition for Endurance Sport: Carbohydrate and Fluid Balance'' by D.L. Costill and J.M. Miller, 1980, *International Journal of Sports Medicine*, 1, p. 2. Copyright 1980. Used by permission.

complex carbohydrates in the form of whole grains, whole grain breads, and fresh fruits and vegetables. These foods, especially whole grains, are excellent sources of such other essential nutrients as protein, vitamins, minerals, fiber, and essential fats. They provide a wealth of CHO for replenishing muscle and liver glycogen.

The concomitant reduction in consumption of high-fat animal products is helpful in maintaining a healthy percentage of body fat and in reducing blood cholesterol levels. Dairy products made with skim milk, lean cuts of meat, white meat poultry and fish, and reduced intake of animal products in general will help you focus on getting enough of the primary fuel source—CHO. These steps will help you eliminate poor nutrition as a cause of poor performance. They will supply your body with ''the right stuff(ing)''—enough carbohydrates for fuel, adequate protein for cell structure, a proper balance of vitamins and minerals for optimal cell function, and enough water and other fluids for all bodily functions. Good nutrition is another tool to help you attain personal bests—in athletics as well as health.

The Carbo Factor: How to Get
the Right Stuff(ing)

It has been well established that CHO is the best fuel to use to replenish the glycogen lost during training. The daily diet must be at least 65% CHO (70-80% during heavy training periods), or there exists the possibility of gradual depletion of muscle and liver glycogen. Side effects of this include chronic fatigue, irritability, injury, and incompletion of planned workouts.

In addition to paying attention to intake percentages, another way exists to obtain enough CHO in your diet. This method involves determining your daily needs in terms of grams of CHO per pound of body weight relative to varying activity levels. Blom, Vaage, and Kardel (1980), after looking at glycogen replenishment rates following exhaustive training, suggested that endurance athletes training at high intensity need to consume between 3.8 and 5.4 grams of CHO per pound of body weight per day in order to maximize glycogen replenishment. This was in the case of athletes who were expending between 3,500 and 5,000 kilocalories per day. Athletes training at lower volumes and intensities will require less CHO per day, usually ranging between 2.5 to 3.8 grams of CHO per pound of body weight. Table 9.1 outlines CHO needs for athletes of various weights and activity levels.

Because most athletes are chronically failing to replenish depleted CHO, the most positive approach to getting enough CHO is to focus on grams of CHO per day. Therefore, it is necessary to become better educated regarding the foods that will give you the most bang for your buck. It's simply a matter of learning which foods to select and how to determine the amount of CHO, protein, and fat in the foods you commonly eat.

Most prepackaged grocery store food items have nutritional information on the package. This can be extremely useful, even though it requires a little bit of translation on your part. Typically, the nutritional information on the package will provide the following information (see Table 9.2):

- Servings per container
- Serving size
- Calories per serving
- Grams of protein
- Grams of carbohydrate
- Grams of fat
- Various other information, such as sodium or vitamin content, and so on

Table 9.1

Daily Carbohydrate Requirements of Endurance Athletes

	Training volumes and intensity			
	Low (3-6 hr/wk)	Moderate (6-8 hr/wk)	High (8-10 hr/wk)	Very high (over 10 hr/wk)
	Grams of carbohydrate needed per day			
Athlete's weight (lb)	2.5 g/lb	2.8 g/lb	3.3 g/lb	3.8 g/lb
100	250	280	330	380
110	275	308	363	418
120	300	336	396	456
130	325	364	429	494
140	350	392	464	532
150	375	420	495	570
160	400	448	528	608
170	425	476	561	646
180	450	504	594	684
190	475	532	627	722
200	500	560	660	760

Note. These values are based on estimates of actual energy expenditure. Variation will depend on the athlete's efficiency of movement and the type of activity employed in training.

The key to deciphering all of this information is knowledge of the energy contribution (in kilocalories) per gram of protein, CHO, and fat. One gram of protein contributes 4 kilocalories, 1 gram of CHO 4 kilocalories, and 1 gram of fat a whopping 9 kilocalories see (Table 9.3). Thus, fat contributes 2¼ times the energy of the same weight of either protein or CHO. For example, a tablespoon of butter, which is 100% fat, provides about 100 kilocalories, the same number of kilocalories as a medium-sized apple, which is 100% CHO.

Therefore, to determine the relative percentages of protein, CHO, and fat in a food item, simply multiply the number of grams of the nutrient by the kilocalorie contribution per gram and divide this result

Table 9.2

Sample Interpretation of Nutritional Information Provided on Food Packaging

Columbo® Blueberry Yogurt	Columbo® Nonfat Lite Raspberry Yogurt
Serving size .... 8 oz	Serving size .... 8 oz
Servings per 1	Servings per 1
Calories 250	Calories 206
Protein .... 8 g	Protein .... 8 g
Carbohydrates .... 38 g	Carbohydrates .... 42 g
Fat .... 7 g	Fat .... 0 g

Note. The regular yogurt is 13.8% protein, 62% CHO, and 24.2% fat, while the Nonfat Lite Yogurt is 16.4% protein, 83.6% CHO, and 0% fat.

into the total kilocalories per serving. For example, one rice cake, which has 66 kilocalories total energy, is 1.4 grams protein, 14 grams CHO, and 0.5 grams fat. Total kilocalories of protein are 5.6 (1.4 × 4 kcals/gram). This means the rice cake's calories are 8.4% protein (5.6 ÷ 66 total calories per serving). Total kilocalories of CHO are 56 (14 X 4 kcals/gram), or 85% of the rice cake's calorie content. Total kilocalories of fat are 4.5 (0.5 X 9 kcals/gram), or 6.8% of the caloric content.

Using this approach while shopping will help you determine which foods are high-fat and which foods are not. It's a good idea to use a nutrition almanac to help with foods, such as meats and cheeses, that do not print nutritional information on the labels. Table 9.4 identifies various healthy foods, their kilocalories per serving, and the grams and percentages of protein, CHO, and fat for comparison to less healthy choices.

One approach I use when giving a lecture on nutrition or working with a group of athletes is what I call the grocery bag technique. I load two grocery bags with food items that have nutritional information on the packages. Then I divide the group into two teams, each receiving a grocery bag. One team gets the "low-fat" bag, and the other group gets the "typical American diet" bag. The teams are instructed to calculate the percentages of protein, CHO, and fat of each food item in the bag. Then they average the percentages of these nutrients for all items, giving the relative percentages of protein, CHO, and fat calories they would get if they ate one serving of each item from their grocery bag that day. The results are usually humorous, and everyone learns a lot about the nutrient content of the foods they eat and how they might substitute food items that are more nutritionally sound, such as using zero-fat yogurt instead of regular yogurt, which can be as high as 40% fat.

Table 9.5 is a list of the top 10 grains, that are over 70% CHO and less than 5% fat and the top 10 legumes, that are over 20% protein and less than 20% fat.

Ultramarathon runner and skier Skip Hamilton seems to have studied this list and taught his daughter, Jennie Ruth, the value of grains. I recently called Skip on the telephone, only to hear his pleasant voice on the answering machine say, "Sorry to miss your call, but Jennie Ruth and I have gone down to the health food store for our daily quota of rolled oats. Gotta keep those carbos up, you know! Leave a message, and I'll get back to you as soon as I can." He might as well have said, "I'll get back to you as soon as my glycogen levels are up."

Table 9.3

Caloric Equivalents of Energy Nutrients

Energy nutrient	Energy (kcal/gram)
Carbohydrate (CHO)	4.1
Protein	4.3
Fat	9.3

Note. Alcohol has a caloric value of 7.1 kcal/gram. However, these calories are considered "empty calories" since they provide no nutritional value in terms of vitamins, minerals, or fiber.

Carbohydrates Before Exercise

There is no need to use the radical "carbo-loading" technique, where you deplete your glygogen stores with exhaustive exercise and low-CHO diets for 3 days, followed by light exercise and a very high-CHO diet for 5 days before competitions. Sherman, Costill, Fink, and Miller (1981) demonstrated that this practice is unnecessary and potentially disruptive and that optimal glycogen storage is accomplished by eating a diet high in CHO every day. Therefore, a constant high-CHO diet is the rule if you wish to maintain and fully replenish glycogen stores.

Table 9.4

Healthy Food Choices for High-CHO Diets

Food	Serving size	Kcals/ serving	CHO (g)	Protein (g)	Fat (g)	% CHO	% Protein	% Fat
Dairy:								
Skim milk	8 oz	100	13	10	<1	52	43	5
Nonfat yogurt	8 oz	200	42	8	0	86	14	0
Low-fat cottage cheese	4 oz	90	3	14	2	14	67	19
Egg whites	1 large	17	.3	3.6	0	7	93	0
Poultry & Fish:								
Chicken breast	3 oz	74	0	14	2.5	0	76	24
Haddock	3 oz	67	0	15.6	.5	0	93	7
Swordfish	3 oz	100	0	16.3	3.4	0	65	35
Tuna (in water)	3 oz	95	0	21	.6	0	88	12
Grains:								
Brown rice (cooked)	8 oz	178	38.2	3.8	1.2	86	8	6
Lentils (cooked)	8 oz	212	38.6	15.6	trace	70	29	1
Kidney beans (cooked)	8 oz	218	39.6	14.4	.9	70	26	4
Spaghetti (cooked)	8 oz	155	32.2	4.8	.6	83	12	3
W. wheat bread	1 slice	56	11	2.4	.7	73	16	11
Rolled oats (cooked)	8 oz	132	23.3	4.8	2.4	69	15	16
Shredded Wheat	1 oz	110	23	3	1	81	11	8
Grape Nuts	1 oz	110	24	3	0	84	16	0
Fruits & Vegetables:								
Apple	1 medium	96	24	.3	0	98	2	0
Banana	1 average	142	33.3	1.6	.3	94	4	2
Potato (baked)	1 large	114	25.7	3.2	.2	90	9	1

Carbohydrates During Exercise: En Route Consumption

The length of the training session or race will determine whether it warrants en route feeds. In general, exercise, particularly intense exercise, lasting over 90 minutes warrants en route consumption. Theoretically, the body will have enough glycogen stored to successfully

Table 9.5

Top Ten Grains and Top Ten
Legumes for Endurance Athletes

Best protein sources: >20% protein and <20% fat	Best carbohydrate sources: >70% carbohydrate and <5% fat
Black beans	Brown rice
Kidney beans	Wild rice
Lima beans	Whole barley
Navy beans	Whole buckwheat
Soybeans	Whole wheat
Black-eyed peas	Rolled oats
Split peas	Whole rye
Dried whole peas	Whole corn
Lentils	Foxtail millet
Wheat germ	Pearl millet

complete any exercise session less than 60 minutes, and even up to 2½ hours if the body is fully loaded with CHO. In practice, as Macaraeg (1983) has demonstrated, en route feedings of scientifically formulated fluid-replacement and energy-drink products during intense exercise delay the onset of exhaustion. (Energy drinks and their benefits will be discussed later in this chapter.) Thus, for exercise sessions or races lasting over 90 minutes, consumption of CHO is recommended to prevent fatigue and restore depleted glycogen.

Carbohydrates After Exercise

In general, the foods you eat after exercise should be the same as those you eat before exercise. However, there are guidelines regarding the time after training at which you should sit down to the table. Depletion of muscle glycogen from training and competition produces an increase in the activity of an enzyme called glycogen synthetase, which raises the muscle cells' receptivity to storing glycogen. Glycogen synthetase activity is most elevated for 2 to 4 hours directly following exercise, and then falls to normal pre-exercise levels within 12 to 24 hours. In other words, carbohydrates are most efficiently converted to stored glycogen immediately following intense exercise.

If you are training hard, it is important to take advantage of this opportunity for glycogen intake. Otherwise, even if you eat a high-CHO diet containing 400 grams CHO per day, you may not fully replenish pre-exercise glycogen levels during peak training periods. For example, if during a training session 50 to 55 millimoles of glycogen per kilogram of muscle tissue is depleted, a CHO-rich diet will restore muscle glycogen in 24 hours. However, if 70 to 80 millimoles of glycogen per kilogram of muscle tissue is depleted, a CHO-rich diet normally will *not* restore muscle glycogen in 24 hours. Thus, although a marathon racer depletes about 150 millimoles of glycogen per kilogram of muscle tissue in a race, only 50 to 60 millimoles of glycogen per kilogram tissue will be replenished in 24 hours. This emphasizes the importance of consuming more CHO soon after long events.

Checklist for CHO Replacement

1. It is best to replace CHO within 2 to 4 hours after training because the enzyme glycogen synthetase will be highest at this point and more of the CHO you eat will be stored.

2. Starches, such as rice, whole grains, breads, pastas, potatoes, fruit, fruit juices, and scientifically formulated energy drinks, seem to be the best forms of CHO for replenishing glycogen during this period right after training.

3. Consumption of a high-CHO diet (65-80% CHO) all the time is the key. If you are eating foods such as pastries, fried foods, ice cream, which contain refined sugars, you are getting some CHO, but you will also be consuming a lot of hidden fats. It is best to eat foods that are not made with oils, butter, or fats—use fresh fruits, sorbets, or low-fat pastries for desserts.

How to Use a Supermarket as a Restaurant

Some supermarkets have delis and salad bars that can provide quick, wholesome carry-out meals for the athlete. Most don't provide these services, however, so it's best to have a strategy for getting nutritious unprepared food at the grocery store. In general, if you stay on the perimeter of the store and refrain from going down most aisles, you'll have good success getting the right stuff. This is because most of the healthier foods—those high in CHO and low in fat—are usually located around the perimeter, in the produce and dairy sections. If you are traveling, it's a good idea to have some utensils and a small bowl on hand, which will allow you to prepare such items as cereal and milk with fruit, sandwiches, or salads. Following is a list of foods to provide you with more menu ideas:

Vegetables: raw carrots, raw celery, salad bar (easy on the dressing!)
Fruit: all fresh fruits, fruit juices, dried fruit, applesauce, jams and jellies
Cereal: Alpen, Familia, muesli, Grape Nuts, Shredded Wheat, Nutri-Grain, rolled oats, Oatios
Milk products: skim milk, zero-fat plain or fruited yogurt, skim-milk cottage cheese
Whole grain breads: Pepperidge Farm whole wheat, Arnold 100% whole wheat, bagels, locally baked whole grain breads
Crackers: Barbara's 100% whole wheat pretzels, Wasa Crispbread, Rykrisp, Kavli Norwegian Flat Bread, rice cakes
Cheese, poultry, fish and legumes: peanut butter, skim-milk cheeses, chicken or turkey breast, tuna in water
Desserts: raisins, Sunshine Raisin Biscuits, fig bars, frozen yogurt, Yodolo, sorbet, frozen fruit bars, bran muffins

Prerace Diets

Experience is the best teacher for finding out what works best for you with regard to your prerace diet. Be sure to test your selected prerace diet in training well before race day. Here are several considerations when planning the prerace diet:

1. For the 10 days preceeding the race—concentrate on increasing your CHO intake to 70% to 80% of your diet's total kilocalories.
2. At 24 hours to race—eat high-CHO, balanced meals with some fiber to eliminate constipation. Hydrate well with water, juices, and energy drinks.
3. At 12 hours to race—reduce intake of solid foods and use more energy drinks. Do not stuff yourself. Use easy-to-digest foods that you have tried in training.
4. At 4 hours to race—consume water or dilute energy drinks. Eat something light if you need to fill your stomach, such as bread, bagels, bananas, and so on. Be certain to experiment with the

foods of choice during hard training sessions or practice races well before race day.

5. At less than 2 hours to race—consume only water or dilute energy drink.

The Fluid Factor

Of all the nutrients to consider, water is the most important. Yet fluid intake often receives inadequate attention.

No matter what your level of sport participation, you have one important similarity to the elite athlete: You will get thirsty. In most adolescents and adults, 60% of the lean body weight is water. Many of the body's functions depend upon water. During vigorous exercise this dependence is pronounced, and the need for fluid replacement becomes crucial. Exercise increases the body's internal core temperature (the temperature around your spine and organs). Vigorous exercise, especially during hot weather, double-session training, or competitions, markedly elevates your core temperature.

Your brain's hypothalamus—the body's thermostat—senses the rise in core temperature and sends messages to the muscles and skin to begin the cooling process. When your hypothalamus senses an increase in core temperature above 37°C, the hot blood at your core moves toward your skin. The sweat mechanism is activated, and the air moving across your damp skin produces the cooling effect of evaporation. Your skin temperature decreases to several degrees below the core temperature, so that hot blood from the core passing through the skin becomes cooler. The blood then moves back to the core to reduce the core temperature, and the cycle continues.

This process costs the body a great deal of precious water. In fact, perspiration is the major cause of water loss. During vigorous activity, such as running, cross-country skiing, cycling, and so on, a person can lose between 1 and 3 liters of water per hour. That can represent a weight loss of up to 7 pounds per hour. If the process continues for an hour or more, the body cannot execute its cooling and other basic functions adequately. Fatigue sets in, and performance is affected. Even relatively mild dehydration reduces performance. Fink (1982) demonstrated that losing only 2% to 3% of the body's fluid through dehydration (about 3 or 4 pounds of body weight) will decrease performance by 3% to 7% in runners competing in 1,500-, 5,000-, and 10,000-meter races. Figure 9.4 illustrates the effects of dehydration on physical performance.

Increased respiration also contributes to dehydration. As the steam from your breath on a cold morning shows, the air you expire contains a good deal of water. You lose more if the air is dry or hot, or

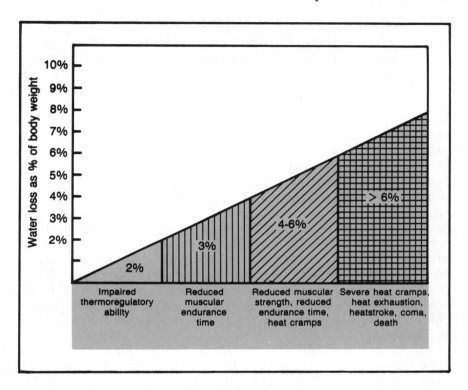

Figure 9.4 Effects of various levels of dehydration on endurance performance.

if you are breathing large volumes of air (as in endurance exercise). During exercise it is possible to lose between 150 milliliters to 300 milliliters of water per hour through respiration alone.

Longer training sessions or competitions mean more water loss. Theoretically, a marathon runner, a triathlete, or a marathon cross-country skier will lose an average of 160 ounces of water over the course of a 2½- to 3-hour race. That's 10 pounds of water! Even if 40 ounces of fluids were consumed along the way, a 120-ounce deficit would remain.

How can you replace so much fluid over the course of the race or practice session? You can't. Your body must be properly hydrated before the event so that you can depend on stored water as well as on water consumed during the race or training session. Stored water is released as follows: For every gram of carbohydrate (glycogen) stored in the muscles, liver, and blood, the body stores 3 to 4 grams of water. During oxidation (combustion) of this glycogen to provide energy, the water is liberated as well and can be used in the cooling process.

This is why athletes who properly hydrate themselves before practice or competition can go the distance without replenishing all fluids lost. Of course, elite athletes can accomplish this more efficiently than average athletes can.

Water will always be a good replenisher. However, commercial sugar-and-electrolyte solutions can be effective if they include appropriate sources of glucose. Macaraeg (1983) has shown that use of polymerized glucose replacement fluids (as compared to no fluids or just plain water) will delay the onset of exhaustion in well-trained athletes (see Figure 9.5). It is best if fluid replacement is a hypotonic solution (one with a lower osmotic pressure than that of the body's fluids). This is necessary to allow adequate absorption during exercise. If the solution is too concentrated, the body will not absorb it well, which might lead to gastric distress and poor assimilation of water. Look for products that use glucose polymer solutions, which are absorbed more completely during exercise. Also, make sure you are familiar with the fluids served at feed stations in any race you enter. If you have not used them before or feel uncomfortable with their concentrations, prepare your own fluids and arrange to have them available. Some basic principles that apply to fluid replacement include the following:

Every day, especially one before competitive or long events, drink eight to ten 8-ounce glasses of water or juice. If you know you need more than that, drink more. One to 2 hours before your event or workout, drink a couple of glasses of water or dilute glucose solution. Drink 5 to 10 ounces of water 10 to 20 minutes before you exercise.

If a competition or workout will last over an hour, it is best to replace fluids every 15 to 20 minutes during exercise. This might mean 5 to 6 ounces of water at every water stop.

It is important not to wait until you are thirsty to drink; if you do so, you will fall far behind your body's water needs. This is why it is so essential to replace water regularly throughout the day as well as during exercise. Your urine color should always be clear. If your urine is chronically cloudy or yellowish in color, you are probably underhydrated (unless you take B-complex vitamins, which give urine a bright greenish-yellow color). Check your urine color frequently and replace fluids appropriately.

Cold water is absorbed faster in your system than warm water is. If you are exercising moderately, this isn't crucial. Furthermore, on a cold day, a warm beverage can feel great. However, on hot days or during intense competition or practice, water must enter your system as fast as possible. Fluid chilled to 40 °F is best suited for this.

The dryness that comes with altitudes above 5,000 feet, coupled with the increased workload the lower partial pressure of oxygen puts on the body, raises fluid requirements. Make sure extra water is available if you live or train at a high altitude.

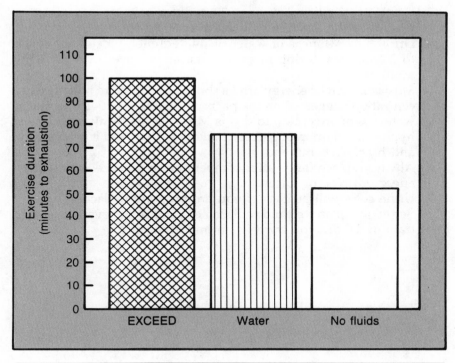

Figure 9.5 Water and fluid replacement energy drinks improve performance. *Note.* From "The Effect of Glucose Polymer-Electrolyte Solution on Exercise Duration" by P.V.J. Macaraeg and C. Abad-Santos. In *Proceedings of Australian Sports Medicine Federation: Medical and Scientific Aspects of Elitism in Sport and Science* (pp. 29-35). Copyright 1984. Reprinted by permission.

After a hard training session or competition, it may take 10 to 20 hours to fully rehydrate your body. If you're planning to exercise hard the next day, rehydrate with water, fruit juices, skim milk, or herb teas. Caffeine drinks such as coffee, tea, or cola, as well as alcohol (such as the postworkout beer) are diuretics (they cause the body to eliminate water) and should be avoided. Check your weight every morning and night to estimate fluid losses; a 5-pound weight loss over 24 hours means you've lost about 2½ quarts of water.

When concerned about losing fluids during training or racing, consider the following guidelines:

1. Drink 8 to 10 glasses of water or juice the day before competition or a long practice.
2. Drink up to 32 ounces of water or diluted energy drink 1 to 2 hours before practice or competition.

3. Drink 1 or 2 glasses of water 20 minutes before competition or practice if the exercise will last over 60 minutes.
4. Drink 3 to 5 ounces of water or diluted energy drink every 15 to 20 minutes during races, events, or practices over 60 to 90 minutes.
5. Most commercial energy drinks should be diluted to half the concentration suggested on the package (that is, use twice as much water). One exception to this is MAX energy drink, which is a hypotonic solution of glucose polymers (I've used it extensively and highly recommend it).
6. Always replace fluids after competition or practice with water, energy drinks, or juices.
7. Urine color will be clear if you are properly replacing fluids.
8. Settle on a plan for fluid replacement and try it several times in training before you try it in an important race.

RESTORATION AS AN INTEGRAL PART OF THE TRAINING PROCESS

S
o far this book has dealt primarily with creating systematic training plans and carrying these plans out in daily activity. Although
these are essential pieces of the total training puzzle, another
component also deserves considerable attention. *Restoration*,
recovery, and *regeneration* can be considered synonyms in this context,
and these terms describe this other, essential component of the training
process.

Athletes and coaches often regard the restoration process to be
adequate if the athlete gets enough sleep at night and has enough
time between workouts to feel fully rested. Little thought goes into
what the athlete actually does during this downtime. Restoration does
not simply refer to this type of general recovery—such as how an athlete feels after a bit of rest. Rather, it refers to the active process of
restoring the muscles and physiological processes that have been
stressed during a specific training session. Additionally, thorough
restoration considers the various psycho-emotional stressors associated
with daily living, such as work, school, personal relationships, or financial problems, and creates a heightened awareness of the effects of
these stressors. Likewise, restoration is not to be confused with rehabilitation from a specific injury, which is a totally different matter.

Consider the training process to be like a balance scale (see Figure 10.1). A small percentage of the time we achieve a stable balance. The rest of the time is spent adding energy to one side or removing it from the other and continually monitoring and checking the balance. It is through this process that we learn. We learn about the effects of various stressors, about their relationship to other factors in life, and ultimately about strategies to use in refining our daily balancing act. Without awareness of and attention to life's stressors, athletes would continue to train full speed ahead, with little regard to the intuitive and learned checks and balances our bodies and minds are capable of administering.

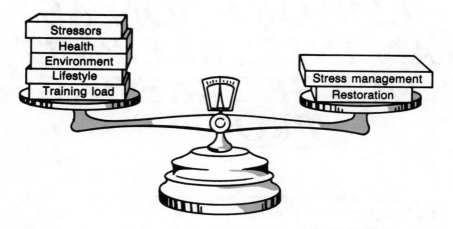

Figure 10.1 Maintaining a balance between the training load/ stressors and restoration processes requires constant awareness of the effects of stressors and the necessary recovery techniques.

As discussed in chapter 3, the body will respond positively to an imposed overload, given the proper restoration processes. However, most athletes' lives involve more than just training and have other stressors that affect restoration. The factors that affect the progress of restoration may occur individually or simultaneously. Although it is beyond the scope of this book to venture into the psycho-emotional ramifications of various stressors, let alone to list the multitude of stressor variables, it is a good idea for you to outline the stress factors that are most common in your life. This will enhance your awareness of how they might affect the training and restoration process. Table 10.1 outlines some of the various factors that can affect recovery and induce a state of overtraining.

Table 10.1

Causes of Overtraining

Training Method

Inappropriate Structure:

- Recovery neglected in weekly and in 4-week cycle periodization pattern
- Too much volume and/or intensity increased too soon
- Too much volume of training at or near AT(threshold intensity)
- Too high an intensity when training for aerobic endurance (OD or Easy Distance)
- Excessive competitions, with associated changes in daily routine and inadequate training time
- Insufficient variety of training methods
- Frequent failure due to setting unrealistic goals

Poor Plan Adjustment to Changing Circumstances:

- Failure to alter training pattern or volume to accommodate other stressors such as work, exams, family, etc.
- Too much training too soon after forced interruptions such as injury or illness

Inappropriate Planning and Teaching Methodology:

- Inadequate knowledge of restoration or stress management or hygeine (i.e., all factors associated with physical and mental health)
- Lack of confidence in training plan or coach
- Too much forced technical instruction that is complicated; not enough opportunity for alternative games and training

Lifestyle

Planning:

- Hurrying things
- Irregular daily routine
- Not enough fun or leisure time (no relaxation)
- Poor quality or insufficient sleep   (Cont.)

Table 10.1 (Continued)

Diet:

- Inadequate balance of carbohydrate, fat, and protein
- Poor fluid replacement
- Excessive alcohol consumption
- Excessive caffeine consumption
- Lack of vitamins and minerals due to poor dietary choices

Housing:

- Poor housing conditions such as noisy, crowded, poor lighting, etc.
- Disturbed home life

Environment

Distractions:

- Continuous conflict with others (family, coach, etc.)
- Inappropriate stimuli (TV, movies, etc.)

Job/Education:

- Unhappy with job
- Time demands of work
- Conflict with others at work
- Overextended in job or school workload
- Low performance in job or school

Personal:

- Tension in family
- Unhappy love relationship
- Family responsibilities

Health

- Allergies
- Asthma
- Colds or flu
- Gastrointestinal problems
- Aftereffects of infectious diseases
- Other chronic problems

Much of the available information regarding training for endurance sports concentrates on appropriate training volumes and methods. Contemporary coaches and athletes usually equate larger training loads with increases in performance, provided that the volume is increased gradually over several years as well as within a given training and competitive season. However, my experience is that most athletes and coaches do not employ a systematic approach to training plans, so that the total training volume is often inappropriate for the individual athlete. Of course, some may follow a "hard-easy" approach to training patterns, alternating high-intensity days with low-intensity days, but few pay close attention to such stress signals as those outlined in chapter 7 (a.m. pulse, a.m. weight, sleep hours, feel of the workout, and completion of the workout).

Restoration and Training Loads

Large training loads (as measured in Year Hours) are indeed necessary for increasing the functional capabilities of the body. Systematically increasing the training volume from year to year as well as within the training year is best accomplished by observing the following:

1. A gradual increase in hours trained per year—usually 5% to 20% per year, depending on your level of development
2. Use of qualified coaching, scientific, and medical assistance, with proper adherence to the training plan and scheduled rest
3. Use of a combination of current training methods and devices, psychological preparation, and effective methods for restoration from training bouts

It is true that the body will improve its ability to recover as part of its adaptation to increased training loads. However, as training programs become more demanding, experienced coaches and sport scientists are finding that recovery time is not keeping pace with increases in training. Therefore, Soviet, German, and Scandinavian sport scientists and coaches have been urging that all training be planned and regulated according to a simple yet thorough restoration program aimed at accelerating the recovery process.

Many world-class endurance athletes train between 700 and 1,000 hours per year. Some athletes in sports such as the triathlon train as much as 8 hours per day! Such training clearly improves race performances. However, as the Soviet coach Zalessky says (quoted in Yessis, 1986), "further increases in physical loads lead to such changes in the athlete that they go beyond physiological norms, worsen the functional state and lower the athlete's capacity for work'' (p. 2). He goes on to say that the most effective way for correcting this is through various restoration methods. Soviet coaches, athletes, and scientists employ a systematic approach to recovery methods, making it possible to increase training load and intensity without injury or overtraining. In fact, a well-thought-out training plan coupled with proper restoration methods actually reduces the incidence of injury.

Planning training so that you recover well from that training is beneficial in several ways. First, the body (and perhaps the mind) recovers more rapidly between training sessions. In other words, the body adapts to the imposed demand more readily. Second, a higher training volume can be sustained, which ultimately will result in higher work capacity. Third, awareness of the effects of stressors is enhanced, making appropriate adjustments to those stressors possible.

The Recovery Process

Yessis (1986) described the recovery process as consisting of three phases: *ongoing recovery*, which happens in the course of a training session; *quick recovery*, which commences at the end of the session and involves metabolic waste removal; and *deep recovery*, which is where adaptation occurs and the athlete's physiological and psychological resources become greater than before. The desired physical improvements seem to depend heavily upon this deep recovery phase.

It takes longer for some bodily systems to recover than it does for others. Connective tissue (tendons and fascia) and supportive tissue (ligaments and bone), because of decreased vascularization, usually take longer to recover than do the metabolic and cardiovascular systems. Likewise, mending of muscle proteins and replenishment of muscle glycogen typically take longer than replenishment of other biochemical substances. It is essential that restoration practices be directed at those systems that require more time to recover.

Muscular acidosis is a primary performance-limiting factor for endurance athletes. As explained before, the feeling of muscle fatigue is caused by accumulations of lactic acid in the muscle tissue. These accumulations can be detected by corresponding increases in blood lactic acid concentrations. Scientists have been analyzing blood lactate in athletes for some time, and these measurements are now routinely used to identify an athlete's state of training and recovery. Several methods for accelerating the clearance of lactate from the musculature have been developed and tested and are used today by athletes and coaches. For example, a simple warm-up and cool-down at easy intensity has been shown to speed removal of metabolic wastes (see chapter 8).

Shevciw (1986) reports that passive methods of recovery can also speed removal of blood lactate. Relaxation baths (water temperature 36 °C) and relaxation massage (30 minutes in length) administered to a group of elite handball players after 30 minutes of vigorous play significantly decreased blood lactate levels in comparison to those found in players who went without regenerative measures after playing. These studies indicate that lactic acid reduction is accelerated when the restorative methods of bath and massage are employed post-exercise.

The overall goal of the training plan and restoration program is to induce the best possible training effect, both physiologically and psychologically, while avoiding overtraining. Overtraining is caused by a host of factors, such as neglect of recovery needs within the training cycle, too much training at or near threshold intensity, an excessive number of competitions, poor planning, poor diet, or stressful living, job, school, or personal situations. However, overtraining can be avoided with the correct restorative methodology.

Restoration Methods

Many restoration methods are currently practiced. The timing and frequency of implementation of the various methods is being researched both clinically and practically. Although it is beyond the scope of this book to offer a conclusive methodology for application of restoration, I will describe several recovery methods currently used by athletes, coaches, and scientists. These are characterized as either *active* or *passive restoration* practices.

Active Restoration

Active restoration involves the physical exertion of the athlete. This is also referred to as *natural restoration*. This category includes the following:

1. Cool-Down Activity

As described in chapter 8, measures such as taking a 15-minute cool-down run seem to improve blood perfusion of muscle tissue, which accelerates removal of lactic acid. The cool-down is usually necessary only after intense efforts, such as Speed, Race/Pace, Interval, Up/Vertical, and Strength training sessions. It is important that the intensity of the cool-down activity be low (at about Level I, described in chapter 5). It has not been definitively determined whether one should actively cool down using the sport activity employed during the training session or whether an alternative activity should be used. Logistically, it might be easiest to extend the workout activity by cooling down using the same, but it may also be beneficial to switch activities for the cool-down. For example, a skier might wish to finish the workout with a 15-minute easy run.

2. Weekly Pattern of the Training Schedule

Typically, a hard day of training, such as Intervals or Race/Pace day, should be followed by an easy day to allow recovery. You can experiment with different weekly patterns depending on the stage of the season, the training volume, and your experience. In general, the more intense the training stage becomes in terms of volume and character of workouts, the greater the need for patterning the week after the hard day-easy day format. You may even wish to employ a hard day-easy day-easy day pattern, allowing 2 easy days between intense days. The benefit of the training session as well as of the active rest may be increased if different equipment, activities, or training environments are planned into the weekly pattern. Cross-training (the use of a variety of sport activities to accomplish a training plan) may decrease stress on the musculoskeletal system, decrease the likelihood of psychological burnout, and increase the restorative capabilities of the body.

3. Fluid Replacement

Fluids, preferably water, must be consumed before, during, and after all training. The urine should be relatively clear and pale. It is a good idea to use an energy drink made with glucose polymers during and after long workouts to replenish lost fluids and carbohydrates at the same time (see chapter 9).

4. Nutrition

The diet must be high in complex carbohydrates, which should be consumed both directly after training and between sessions. The muscle glycogen depleted during training can best be replenished in this manner. Also, recommended daily allowances of trace minerals, such as iron, zinc, chromium, selenium, calcium, potassium, sodium, and magnesium, which are necessary for normal biochemical reactions, should be consumed as part of the foods selected (see chapter 9).

5. Sleep

Normal sleep amounts and patterns need to be maintained, particularly during high-intensity training periods. Bedtime and hours of sleep should be consistent if possible, and the bed should be comfortable and firm. If two training sessions are planned in one day, naps between workouts, if time allows, may be beneficial in promoting recovery.

6. Walking

Simple walks, taken with an attitude of leisure and relaxation, may be useful in restoration. Usually evening walks after the day's training sessions are most effective.

Passive Restoration

Passive restorative techniques do not require your active physical involvement. There are many passive methods of restoration therapy. The relaxation bath and the relaxation massage are particularly popular in sport applications.

1. Massage

Perhaps one of the most widely used methods for recovery is massage (Figure 10.2). Massage can take many forms, and several techniques are popular with and useful for athletes. Proper massage accelerates recovery from workouts and can increase your total work capacity. The increased blood flow to the muscles during massage promotes lactate removal and nourishment of the muscle tissue.

Sport massage by a qualified professional is perhaps the most effective, but most athletes lack the necessary financial resources for or access to massage therapy. However, considerable benefit can be derived from self-massage techniques. The main techniques for self-massage involve jostling, kneading, and stroking the muscles with slow, soft movements directly after a workout or competition. Self-massage can be used several hours after the workout as well, when it typically is longer in duration. For more information about massage, refer to the recommended readings that appear near the end of this book.

2. Relaxation Baths

These are one of the oldest known forms of restoration. It is on record that Aristotle enjoyed relaxation baths. However, it is not clearly known how baths work to regenerate the body. They seem to promote blood circulation and muscle relaxation. Whirlpool or Jacuzzi hot tubs, with water at 36 °C (96.8 °F) effectively accelerate blood lactate removal and heart rate recovery.

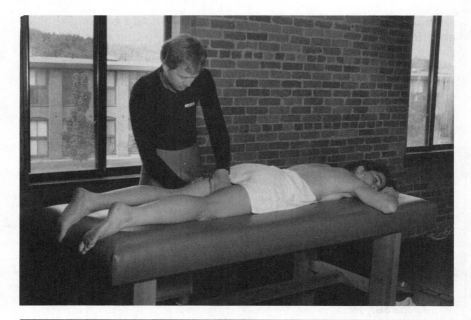

Figure 10.2 Sports massage can reduce recovery time between training bouts.

3. Progressive Muscle Relaxation

Relaxation of the muscles can be enhanced by employing learned techniques for progressively reducing muscle tension. A variety of techniques may be used, including self-hypnosis, visualization, and muscle tensing and releasing. Qualified professionals are recommended for teaching these techniques, which can be learned by audiotape or in person. The benefits are improved blood circulation, speedier removal of metabolic wastes, and improved nourishment of tissue by nutrients in the blood.

4. Other Methods

The Soviets report very sophisticated methods for restoration, including massage during workouts; various water procedures, such as showers, saunas, and baths (Figures 10.3 and 10.4); ultrasound and electrostimulation; autogenic psychoregulation relaxation therapy; and special pharmacologically derived diet and fluid-replacement therapies. Many of these procedures require careful administration and monitoring and may be logistically difficult for the average citizen racer to employ.

Figure 10.3 Sauna baths are a fun way to relax and speed up the restoration process.

Figure 10.4 Many top athletes use the jacuzzi as part of a complete recovery plan.

Over the past 2 years, the U.S. Biathlon Men's Elite Team has employed an extensive restoration program. The typical daily recovery plan included the following order of activities:

After a.m. training:

1. Cool-down of 15 to 45 minutes, depending on workout intensity
2. Warm shower
3. Light massage for 20 to 30 minutes
4. High-carbohydrate meal and fluid replacement
5. Nap or relaxation training

After p.m. Training:

1. Cool-down
2. Warm shower
3. Specific massage 30 to 60 minutes in duration, 2 to 6 hours after training
4. High-carbohydrate meal and fluid replacement
5. Sauna or whirlpool alternated with cool shower
6. Relaxation training, if necessary

Although it is difficult to objectively measure the results of such a program, these athletes are now training at higher yearly volumes than before, with fewer incidences of injury, and with marked improvement in international competition.

However, most athletes find it impossible to incorporate so many passive recovery methods into their training. The active recovery methods described may be more practical. You and your coach must consider them an integral part of the training session. The stress monitors described in chapter 7, if tracked accurately and recorded in a meaningful training log, may greatly enhance the use of these recovery procedures.

Feel Better—Have More Fun

Restoration from training may give you an extra edge, both physiologically and psychologically. It is also an extension of taking good care of yourself. This helps you feel better about yourself, your training, and others around you. It helps you maintain a balance in training and in your life. Ultimately, you'll train better, feel better, perform better, and, hopefully, have more fun with training and competitions.

CHAPTER 11

PUTTING IT ALL TOGETHER: SKILLS FOR EFFECTIVE TRAINING MANAGEMENT

E ven the best athletes must make adjustments to their training plans, sometimes frequently. It would be nice to think that once carefully planned, your training program will progress without mishap. However, most people will need to make adjustments to their training plans to accommodate a variety of factors. This chapter is devoted to highlighting the possible adjustments you may need to make and strategies for making positive changes in the plan. Also included is a checklist for approaching training sessions and competitions.

Adjustments in Your Training Plan

There are two basic ways to make adjustments in your training plan. The first is by changing the basic structure of the plan in terms of weekly patterns, periodization, volume of training per cycle, percentages of SERIOUS components per cycle, and yearly volume. The second type of adjustment is made on a daily or weekly basis and deals primarily with reacting to stressful circumstances, such as illness, overtime at work, relationship problems, or travel.

Varying the Plan's Structure

The worksheets presented in chapter 6 can be used to make any fundamental changes in the structure of the plan and to observe the effects these changes have on the entire program. For example, if you change the periodization pattern in one cycle, you can see the effect in the next cycle in terms of how well you recover between cycles. If you decide that you need a greater percentage of Speed work in a cycle, you can see the effective change in that cycle and, more importantly, attempt to observe and measure the effect of that change in your speed on race day.

Adjusting one variable in a systematic plan does affect the other variables to some degree. The following are areas you might be likely to adjust:

Yearly Volume (Year Hours)

Most likely you will need to decrease volume due to an overly ambitious goal set during planning stages or to changes in available time per week because of school workload, job commitments, family commitments, or other factors. Sometimes an increase in volume is necessary. The rule is to increase volume by 5% to 10% maximum. If adjusting volume is the only change to your plan, the calculations will be easy because you'll use the original template as is.

Percentage of Total Volume per Cycle

Sometimes an increase or decrease in volume within a single cycle is necessary because of other commitments. If such changes are made, all the other cycles must change in their percentages of total year volume as well in order to maintain a total value of 100%.

Periodization Patterns

Not all the answers are known regarding the best periodization pattern for each training cycle. It is important to follow basic guidelines that have been successfully used by others, such as the periodization patterns presented in chapter 6. However, it is a good idea to experiment with different patterns to find what works best for you and what may work for a particular time period. For example, if races occur every 2 weeks in a cycle, you might adopt a hard week-easy week format for the cycle, with races falling on the ends of the easy weeks (e.g., a periodization pattern of 30-20-30-20). There are many ways to shape the periodization of a cycle, and these should be experimented with in regard to stage of year, volume per cycle, and so on.

Percentage of SERIOUS Components

Again, not all the answers are known regarding the percentages of the various training components used in a given cycle and stage. An experienced athlete who has built a strong base over the years may have considerable success using a greater percentage of higher intensity training than a lesser trained athlete would. Undoubtedly, new training theories will arise. By using a systematic approach, you can effectively incorporate these into your basic structure and then measure the effects of these changes by race performances and subjective feelings.

Varying Daily and Weekly Plans

The second way to adjust your plan involves changing it on a daily or weekly basis by monitoring stressors due to various life circumstances. It is important to be prepared to skip a workout or reduce the time allotment of a scheduled workout. The following are some ideas on when and how to make these changes:

Stress Monitors

The stress monitors used in the log system outlined in chapter 7 can be extremely helpful for monitoring progress as well as for detecting early signs of fatigue or overtraining. For example, if your morning pulse is 20% higher than normal, your weight 4% lower than normal, and your urine very concentrated, it would be a good idea if you (a) started drinking a lot of water and (b) chose not to do a planned 60-minute hard Interval session. Instead, you might reduce the time by half, do the workout at easy intensity, or even take the day off until you feel recovered. You should also try to understand why your body expressed those stress signals in the first place. Perhaps that analysis would give you a new perspective on your overall plan so you could make adjustments accordingly.

Life's Circumstances

Schoolwork; job projects or overtime; relationship difficulties; financial pressure; conflicts with friends, co-workers, employers, or family; travel; poor diet; low-quality sleep; and unexpected illness all have their effect on the body, and it is difficult to measure the effects objectively. The stress monitors just described can help in many cases. However, you may not be able to put your finger on a cause for feeling low. In these cases, sometimes it is best just to take a day off from training or to change the training environment or activity. Be prepared to make adjustments based on how you feel. There is no need to become a slave to your plan. If you miss a training session or if you decide to take a day or more off, take the rest willingly and don't try to make up for it later—you'll only make matters worse. Just pick up with your plan on the next day or workout.

Unrealistic Goals

Many of us set lofty goals for performance. The risk is that we may set ourselves up for disappointment if we don't meet our expectations. Be ready to adjust your goals to accommodate your training program, and set realistic expectations for improvement. Talk with a coach or someone who knows you well regarding your goals. They may help you see your expectations more objectively.

Cross-Training for Variety and Fun

Just as you'll need to make adjustments occasionally, you may find it helpful to use variety in accomplishing your training plan. The use of different activities occasionally (or often, if you're a triathlete or a cross-country skier in dryland training) will keep your body fresh as well as stimulate your mind. Runners may try an easy cross-country ski tour or a water-running workout, both of which are very similar motions to running yet induce less musculoskeletal trauma than running does.

It's a good idea to vary the training environment often, using unfamiliar territory occasionally. It's also a good idea to recruit a different training partner once in a while. It can be refreshing, and you might learn something from the other person.

Allow yourself some unstructured training occasionally. Play soccer, ultimate frisbee, volleyball, or tennis with little regard to intensity. If you feel you need to fit this play into your plan somehow, take the time allotment from an Endurance/Easy Distance workout. Another way to accomplish unstructured training is to leave your watch and your pulse monitor at home and go fast when you want to, rest when you want to, and go easy when it feels right—do whatever comes to mind. *Fartlek* means speed play, and the originators, the Scandinavians, knew how to play. A run through the woods might include pullups on a tree limb, a swimming interlude followed by a rest in the sun, then a short, hard run up a hill, some calisthenics, and finally home, skipping all the way! Allow the child in you to have fun.

Commonsense Approach to Training and Competitions

You should be well prepared, both before stepping up to the starting line at a race and before each training session. The adage "work smarter, not harder" has significant meaning to the runner who finishes a race only to learn that he was disqualified because he took a wrong turn because he did not review the course, or to the cyclist who learns that a skintight Lycra suit could have meant a significant time improvement in a bike race. Preparation for racing involves using good sense to eliminate any barriers to your optimal performance. The following sections offer some things to consider in planning for competition.

Race Preparation Checklist

Nothing beats experience for being totally prepared for a race. However, there have been many cases where an experienced athlete goofed. For example, I know of one National Team skier who, at the National Championships, grabbed the wrong pair of skis as she ran to the starting line. She didn't realize her mistake until it was too late. Wrong wax, wrong skis, bad race!

You may find it helpful to write down a checklist and practice a few times before race day. Include equipment, clothing, registration, bib numbers, food and water before and during the race, medical problems, enough sleep, and enough time before the race to do a proper warm-up and check. Basically, assume that you will be responsible for doing everything and leave nothing to chance. It's a bit disheartening, for example, to jump on your bike in a triathlon only to realize that you forgot to fill your water bottle. The bottom line is that you want to eliminate any surprises. Be familiar with everything, yet be prepared to make a change if necessary.

Course Review

Take the time, either the day before or in the weeks preceding competition, to review the course. Study the areas that might be troublesome or that will be the best for making your move. Ideally, it is best to do a complete time trial on the course at some point 3 weeks or longer before the race. If you cannot do this, then try to get to the race early enough to drive the course, if appropriate, or review course maps and profiles and talk with someone about aid stations and other logistical considerations.

Body Composition and Performance

In general, an ideal percentage of body fat will be beneficial for every endurance athlete. Elite male endurance athletes have body fat percentages ranging between 3% and 8% and elite women between 8% and 18%. Extra fat is extra baggage that you must carry up hills against gravity. Imagine carrying a 10-pound pack up a hill in a race. It would require a lot of extra energy expenditure. This is especially true in distance running. In other sports, fat is added insulation that makes it more difficult for the body to cool itself. (However, some body fat is necessary for normal physiological functions and insulation from the cold, especially in skiing and swimming.) If you want to eliminate extra body fat, you need a plan for losing the excess. Following the diet recommendations in chapter 9 will supply the foods that promote a lean physique and fuel your endurance engine.

Have your body fat measured. The quickest and most convenient way to do this is with body fat calipers, which measure the skinfold thickness at various spots on the body (Figure 11.1). However, to obtain the most accurate skinfold test results, go to a qualified professional, such as an exercise physiologist or physician who has been trained in the technique and who knows which calculation to use for your age, gender, and sport. The other commonly accepted method is hydrostatic (underwater) weighing. It is presently considered the "gold standard" for accuracy in assessing body fat percentage. Many human performance laboratories and sports medicine clinics have the equipment for this test. You are weighed underwater and your body fat is calculated based on body density. In general, the less fat you have and the more lean you are, the more you weigh underwater (for a given size).

If you find that you need to lose body fat, lose it slowly by decreasing your daily caloric intake, using a high-carbohydrate, low-fat diet, and increasing your training volume slightly. Plan to lose only ½ to 1 pound of fat per week, beginning 6 to 9 months before the racing season.

Diet and Fluid Replacement

The guidelines in chapter 9 outline what are generally best to eat and drink. However, regarding race-day food and drink consumption prior

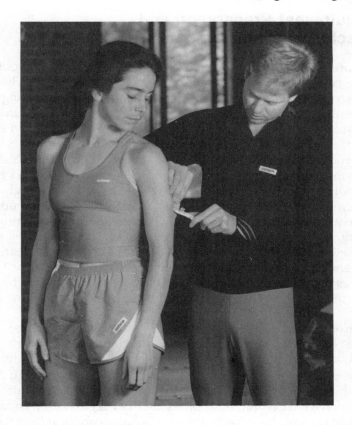

Figure 11.1 An accurate assessment of your body fat percentage is the best way to determine whether you need to lose fat weight. Excess body fat is just extra baggage for the endurance athlete.

to the start, it's a good idea to know exactly what works and what doesn't work for you. The best way to find out what works is to try it out in training. If you are planning to use an energy drink on race day, be sure to use it under similar conditions during a training Pace workout or in a race that is not very important to you. It's risky to drink something during a race that you have not used before. Plan to have a friend out on the course with fluids you have prepared in advance, or carry your own, as many cyclists, triathletes, and skiers do with special bottle racks and fanny packs.

The same applies to prerace diets. Try them out well before race day. It's a good idea to determine whether you'll need to have something in your stomach a certain number of hours before the start and also to know the start time relative to your usual eating patterns. Again, the goal is to eliminate surprises so you can focus on the race.

Equipment Preparation and Technical Considerations

There are many ways to increase overall performance without costing the body more energy. Some may even save energy. The main thing is to adopt an attitude of investigation and problem solving when considering your equipment, clothing, gadgets, and training methods and tests. As author George Sheehan states, "We are each an experiment of one." So, let the experiment commence.

Aerodynamic gear and clothing has become one of the latest rages in shaving seconds, even minutes, off performance times in endurance sports. Speed skaters were among the first to don skintight Lycra bodysuits and hoods. Swimmers have long been shaving body hair to decrease resistance in the water. Cyclists are experimenting with clothing, helmets, and most significantly, bicycles themselves. At racing speeds of over 20 mph on a level course, a cyclist uses nearly 90% of expended energy overcoming wind resistance. Wind resistance increases proportionally to the square of speed. Much testing has been conducted to prove that lower wind drag means faster times. This principle applies for all sports.

Aerodynamic objects are shaped like sleek aircraft or tear drops; they leave the air fairly undisturbed as they pass through. Blunt shapes, such as squares, cylinders, or spheres, are not aerodynamic, because they create large-scale turbulence as they pass through the air.

Although it is necessary to reduce wind resistance in our equipment, such as in cycling, our bodies are our biggest aerodynamic liabilities. In cycling, for example, the body causes about 70% of the total wind drag, the bicycle 30%. Therefore, improvements in the human form will achieve the greatest effectiveness (Figure 11.2). You can make major improvements simply by using aerodynamically efficient clothing. Loose shorts, shirts, or suits that flutter in the wind or drag in the water increase air and water friction enormously. Tight, sleek suits allow for smooth airflow over the body. Cycling researchers claim that a tight Spandex suit lowers wind resistance nearly 6% as compared to standard cotton or wool clothing. Lycra Spandex is also lighter and cooler than cotton or wool garments. Skiers, cyclists, triathletes, and swimmers all benefit from using this type of suit. Skiers and cyclists probably need to consider Lycra boot covers and gloves, which are also "slippery" in the air.

Chet Kyle, PhD, a researcher in mechanical engineering at California State University at Long Beach, led the research team that developed equipment for the 1984 American Olympic cyclists. Among Kyle's findings was, surprisingly, how much hair slows a cyclist down. He found that long or bushy hair has a very high wind drag—thus the importance of using aerodynamic helmets in cycling. Teardrop-shaped helmets are being used regularly by many elite cyclists and triathletes.

Figure 11.2 Top cyclist Jack Nash uses an aerodynamically designed "funny bike," lycra suit, and helmet for competing in time trials. Note his low body position as he leans over the handlebars.

Cross-country skiers would be well advised to try a full-body, head-to-toe Lycra suit similar to those used by speed skaters. Typically, skiers wear wool or polypropylene hats with tassels and much of the cloth loose and overhanging, or no hat at all. Swimmers should shave body hair and use swim caps.

Equipment technology's quest for aerodynamic efficiency has yielded some effective products. Again, cycling has led the way, developing aerodynamic bike frames, handlebars, water bottles, cranks, pedals, 24-inch front wheels, more slippery spoked wheels, and disk wheels—all of which can shave many seconds, even minutes, off your race times. Cross-country skiing technology has produced stiffer boot-and-binding combinations for ski-skating, faster skis, new poles, faster waxes, and, in the Biathlon, lighter rifles. It is beyond the scope of this book to describe the benefits of these in detail. However, you should be aware of these factors and use them to your advantage, with due consideration of your goals and your pocketbook.

Recently, however, while attending a local triathlon, I was reminded to keep all of this in perspective. As I observed many of the racers' aerodynamic gear—helmets, disk wheels, skintight suits—one racer came chugging by on his old, heavy clunker of a bike, wearing running shoes with holes in them, old khaki shorts, and a T-shirt flapping in the wind. He had a grin from ear to ear as he rode past many of the "sleek" athletes!

Clothing and equipment have a purely functional purpose. Footwear must be comfortable and must be replaced frequently to avoid injuries that can occur as a result of inadequate cushioning or support. Wetsuits give swimmers and triathletes greater buoyancy as well as more comfortable training in colder water, resulting in better workouts and races. Cyclists using padded bike shorts, windproof jerseys, eye goggles, and padded gloves will beat the effects of weather on long rides. Some runners are beating overuse injuries with hydrotraining. Ask yourself about the function of the equipment you are using, whether it will prevent overuse injuries, and whether you can afford to upgrade your gear.

Moving Ahead

Remember that a training plan is only as good as the work that goes into creating, maintaining, and adjusting it. The smart athlete or coach will continually make assessments regarding training progress and recovery. Be prepared to make changes when necessary, especially if the changes can be based on accurate information gathered with the training log and by stress-monitor factors.

Use a commonsense approach with training, diet, fluids, equipment, and race preparation. Let there be no surprises on race day due to your poor planning and preparation. Yet, be ready to make adjustments on race day according to the variables that can change.

APPENDIX A

SYSTEMATIC TRAINING PLAN WORKSHEETS

WORKSHEET A.1:
Objectives of the overall year plan

Training plan for the year 19 _____

Name _____

1 Events and competitions _____

_____

2	Performance goals	
3	Physical preparation	
4	Psychological preparation	
5	Technical preparation	
6	Tests & standards	

WORKSHEET A.2:
Determination of each 4-week cycle's character

Training plan for the year _____
Name _____
1 Year hours to train _____

Cycle	**2** Date	**3** Stage	**3** Emphasis	**4** % Year hours	**5** Periodization % Weeks			
					1	2	3	4
1								
2								
3								
4								
5								
6								
7								
8								
9								
10								
11								
12								
13								

WORKSHEET A.3:
Determination of the percentage of training
components per 4-week cycle

Training plan for the year _____
Name _____

Cycle	**1** Stage	**2** Percentage of hours	Percentage per 4-week cycle						
			3 Speed	Endurance	Race/Pace	Interval	Overdistance	Up/Vertical	Strength
1									
2									
3									
4									
5									
6									
7									
8									
9									
10									
11									
12									
13									

WORKSHEET A.4: Training Plan for the Year—Spreadsheet Calculations

Training plan for the year 19____

Name ____

Projected year hours to train ____

	Four-week cycle	1				2				3				4				5			
1	Four-week cycle	1				2				3				4				5			
2	Training stage																				
	Week numbers	1 - 4				5 - 8				9 - 12				13 - 16				17 - 20			
3	Actual dates																				
4	% of year hours																				
5	Actual hours/cycle																				
	Actual week number	1	2	3	4	5	6	7	8	9	10	11	12	13	14	15	16	17	18	19	20
6	Periodization pattern																				
7	Actual hours/week																				
8	Speed																				
	Endurance																				
	Race/Pace																				
	Intervals																				
	Overdistance																				
	Up/Vertical																				
	Strength																				

WORKSHEET A.4, continued

		6				7				8				9		
1	Four-week cycle															
2	Training stage															
	Week numbers	21 - 24				25 - 28				29 - 32				33 - 36		
3	Actual dates															
4	% of year hours															
5	Actual hours/cycle															
	Actual week number	21	22	23	24	25	26	27	28	29	30	31	32	33	34	35	36
6	Periodization pattern															
7	Actual hours/week															
8	Speed															
	Endurance															
	Race/Pace															
	Intervals															
	Overdistance															
	Up/Vertical															
	Strength															

(cont.)

WORKSHEET A.4, continued

	Four-week cycle	10				11				12				13			
1	Four-week cycle	10				11				12				13			
2	Training stage																
	Week numbers	37–40				41–44				45–48				49–52			
3	Actual dates																
4	% of year hours																
5	Actual hours/cycle																
	Actual week number	37	38	39	40	41	42	43	44	45	46	47	48	49	50	51	52
6	Periodization pattern																
7	Actual hours/week																
8	Speed																
	Endurance																
	Race/Pace																
	Intervals																
	Overdistance																
	Up/Vertical																
	Strength																

WORKSHEET A.5:
Determining the Weekly Pattern for Each 4-Week Cycle

1 Training cycle #		2 Actual dates of cycle					
					Week # & date		
Day	3 Objective	4 Sport	5 Intensity	6 Time (in minutes) per workout			
1A							
B							
2A							
B							
3A							
B							
4A							
B							
5A							
B							
6A							
B							
7A							
B							

(cont.)

WORKSHEET A.5: Continued

Typical weekly patterns and associated percentage of training components for base, intensity, peak, and race stages of the training year (based on percent of total time allotment per training component)

Day	Base Objective	%	Intensity Objective	%	Peak Objective	%	Racing Objective	%
1A	OD	50	OD	50	OD	50	OD	50
B	OFF		OFF		OFF		OFF	
2A	EN	33	UP	100	UP	100	OFF	
B	ST	33	ST	50	ST	100	OFF	
3A	OD	25	OD	25	OD	25	OD	25
B	OFF		OFF		SP	50	SP	50
4A	EN	33	IN	100	IN	100	IN	100
B	ST	33	ST	50	OFF		OFF	
5A	OD	25	OD	25	OD	25	OD	25
B	OFF		SP	100	SP	100	SP	100
6A	EN	33	EN	100	EN	100	EN	100
B	ST	33	OFF		OFF		OFF	
7A	OFF		RP	100	RP	100	RP	100
B	OFF		OFF		OFF		OFF	

SP = Speed
EN = Endurance
RP = Race/Pace
IN = Intervals

OD = Overdistance
UP = Up/Vertical
ST = Strength

APPENDIX B

WORKSHEET TEMPLATES FOR SPECIFIC SPORTS

Templates

Worksheet B.1:   Triathlon—Beginner to USTS Distance, One Competitive Season per Year

Worksheet B.2:   Triathlon—Ironman Distances, One Competitive Season per Year

Worksheet B.3:   Running—5, 10, 15 km, One Competitive Season per Year

Worksheet B.4:   Marathon, One Competitive Season per Year

Worksheet B.5:   Cycling—Criteriums, Short Road Races, Time Trials, One Competitive Season per Year

Worksheet B.6:   Cycling—Longer Road Races, One Competitive Season per Year

Worksheet B.7:   Cross-Country Skiing—5-35 km, One Competitive Season per Year

Worksheet B.8:   Cross-Country Skiing—25-50 km, One Competitive Season per Year

Worksheet B.9:   Two Competitive Seasons per Year—Cross-Country Skiing, 10-50 km, Weeks 1-24; Triathlon, USTS to Ironman, Weeks 25-52

Worksheet B.10:   Two Competitive Seasons per Year—Cross-Country Skiing, 10-50 km, Weeks 1-24; Cycling, Road Races, Weeks 25-52

Worksheet B.11:   Two Competitive Seasons per Year—Running, 10 km, Weeks 1-24; Running, Marathon, Weeks 25-52

Instructions

The templates in Appendix B are formatted differently from the worksheets in Appendix A and chapter 6. Following these steps will help you use the sport-specific templates more easily:

Step 1: Determine the Year Hours you will use for the plan. Enter in (A).

Step 2: Determine the dates of each 4-week training cycle. Enter in (B).

Step 3: Multiply the percentage of Year Hours per cycle (C) by total Year Hours (A) for each cycle. Enter in (D).

Step 4: Multiply the result of Step 3, actual hours per cycle (D), by the periodization pattern percentages (F) for each week of every cycle. Enter in (G).

Step 5: Multiply the result of Step 4, actual hours per week (G), by percentages of each SERIOUS training component per cycle (E). Enter in each SERIOUS training component space (H).

Note: To determine weekly training patterns for scheduling the training times from Step 5, refer to chapter 6, Worksheet 6.5 for assistance.

WORKSHEET B.1: Triathlons—Beginner to USTS Distances, One Competitive Season per Year

Training plan for the year 19____   Name _____   **1** Projected year hours to train (A) ____

	Four-week cycle	1	2	3	4	5
	Training stage	BASE	BASE	BASE	BASE	INTENSITY
	Week numbers	1 - 4	5 - 8	9 - 12	13 - 16	17 - 20
2	Actual dates (B)					
	% of year hours (C)	7	7	7.5	8	8.5
3	Actual hrs/cycle (D)					
Percent per cycle	Speed (E)	0	0	0	0	0
	Endurance	10	10	10	10	10
	Race/Pace	0	0	0	0	0
	Intervals	0	0	0	5	5
	Overdistance	70	70	70	65	60
	Up/Vertical	0	0	0	5	10
	Strength	20	20	20	15	15

	Actual week number	1	2	3	4	5	6	7	8	9	10	11	12	13	14	15	16	17	18	19	20
	Periodization (%) (F)	23	26	29	22	23	26	29	22	23	26	29	22	23	26	29	22	22	27	33	18
4	Actual hrs/week (G)																				
5	Speed (H)																				
Hours per week	Endurance																				
	Race/Pace																				
	Intervals																				
	Overdistance																				
	Up/Vertical																				
	Strength																				

WORKSHEET B.1, continued

Four-week cycle	6	7	8	9
Training stage	INTENSITY	INTENSITY	INTENSITY	PEAK
Week numbers	21 - 24	25 - 28	29 - 32	33 - 36
2 Actual dates (B)				
% of year hours (C)	9	9.5	10	8
3 Actual hrs/cycle (D)				
Speed (E)	5	5	5	10
Endurance	5	5	5	10
Race/Pace	5	5	5	10
Intervals	10	10	10	15
Overdistance	60	60	60	50
Up/Vertical	5	5	5	0
Strength	10	10	10	5

Percent per cycle (Speed through Strength)

Actual week number	21	22	23	24	25	26	27	28	29	30	31	32	33	34	35	36
4 Periodization (%) (F)	22	27	33	18	22	27	33	18	22	27	33	18	22	27	33	18
5 Actual hrs/week (G)																
Speed (H)																
Endurance																
Race/Pace																
Intervals																
Overdistance																
Up/Vertical																
Strength																

Hours per week (Actual hrs/week through Strength)

(cont.)

WORKSHEET B.1, continued

Four-week cycle	10	11	12	13
Training stage	RACE	RACE	RACE	RESTORATION
Week numbers	37 - 40	41 - 44	45 - 48	49 - 52
Actual dates (B)				
% of year hours (C)	7	7	6.5	5
Actual hrs/cycle (D)				
Speed (E)	10	10	10	0
Endurance	5	5	5	40
Race/Pace	15	15	15	0
Intervals	15	10	10	0
Overdistance	50	55	55	60
Up/Vertical	0	0	0	0
Strength	5	5	5	0

2 — 3 Percent per cycle

Actual week number	37	38	39	40	41	42	43	44	45	46	47	48	49	50	51	52
Periodization (%) (F)	30	20	30	20	30	20	30	20	30	20	30	20	25	25	25	25
Actual hrs/week (G)																
Speed (H)																
Endurance																
Race/Pace																
Intervals																
Overdistance																
Up/Vertical																
Strength																

4 — 5 Hours per week

WORKSHEET B.2: Triathlon—Ironman Distances, One Competitive Season per Year

Training plan for the year 19____   Name _____

[1] Projected year hours to train (A) _____

Four-week cycle	1	2	3	4	5
Training stage	BASE	BASE	BASE	BASE	INTENSITY
Week numbers	1 - 4	5 - 8	9 - 12	13 - 16	17 - 20
Actual dates (B)					
% of year hours (C)	6	7	8	9	9
Actual hrs/cycle (D)					
[2] Speed (E)	0	0	0	0	5
Endurance	10	10	5	10	5
Race/Pace	0	0	0	0	0
Intervals	0	0	0	5	5
Overdistance	70	70	70	65	60
Up/Vertical	0	0	5	5	10
Strength	20	20	20	15	15

(Percent per cycle)

Actual week number	1	2	3	4	5	6	7	8	9	10	11	12	13	14	15	16	17	18	19	20
Periodization (%) (F)	23	26	29	22	23	26	29	22	23	26	29	22	23	26	29	22	22	27	33	18
[4] Actual hrs/week (G)																				
[5] Speed (H)																				
Endurance																				
Race/Pace																				
Intervals																				
Overdistance																				
Up/Vertical																				
Strength																				

(Hours per week)

(cont.)

WORKSHEET B.2, continued

	6	7	8	9
Four-week cycle				
Training stage	INTENSITY	INTENSITY	INTENSITY	PEAK
Week numbers	21 - 24	25 - 28	29 - 32	33 - 36
2 Actual dates (B)				
% of year hours (C)	10	11	9	8
3 Actual hrs/cycle (D)				
Speed (E)	5	5	5	10
Endurance	5	5	5	10
Race/Pace	5	5	5	10
Intervals	8	10	10	15
Overdistance	60	60	60	50
Up/Vertical	7	5	5	0
Strength	10	10	10	5

(Percent per cycle)

	21	22	23	24	25	26	27	28	29	30	31	32	33	34	35	36
Actual week number	21	22	23	24	25	26	27	28	29	30	31	32	33	34	35	36
Periodization (%) (F)	22	27	33	18	22	27	33	18	22	27	33	18	22	27	33	18
4 Actual hrs/week (G)																
5 Speed (H)																
Endurance																
Race/Pace																
Intervals																
Overdistance																
Up/Vertical																
Strength																

(Hours per week)

WORKSHEET B.2, continued

	10				11				12				13			
Four-week cycle	10				11				12				13			
Training stage	RACE				RACE				RACE				RESTORATION			
Week numbers	37 - 40				41 - 44				45 - 48				49 - 52			
Actual dates (B) [2]																
% of year hours (C)	7				7				6				3			
Actual hrs/cycle (D) [3]																
Speed (E)	10				10				10				0			
Endurance	5				5				5				40			
Race/Pace	15				15				15				0			
Intervals	15				10				10				0			
Overdistance	50				55				55				60			
Up/Vertical	0				0				0				0			
Strength	5				5				5				0			
(Percent per cycle)																
Actual week number	37	38	39	40	41	42	43	44	45	46	47	48	49	50	51	52
Periodization (%) (F)	30	20	30	20	30	20	30	20	30	20	30	20	25	25	25	25
Actual hrs/week (G) [4]																
Speed (H) [5]																
Endurance																
Race/Pace																
Intervals																
Overdistance																
Up/Vertical																
Strength																
(Hours per week)																

WORKSHEET B.3: Running—5, 10, 15 km, One Competitive Season per Year

Training plan for the year 19____   Name _____   **[1]** Projected year hours to train (A) ____

	1	2	3	4	5	6	7	8	9	10	11	12	13	14	15	16	17	18	19	20
Four-week cycle	1				2				3				4				5			
Training stage	BASE				BASE				BASE				BASE				INTENSITY			
Week numbers	1 - 4				5 - 8				9 - 12				13 - 16				17 - 20			
Actual dates (B)																				
% of year hours (C)	7				7				7.5				8				8.5			
Actual hrs/cycle (D)																				

[2] Percent per cycle

	1	2	3	4	5	6	7	8	9	10	11	12	13	14	15	16	17	18	19	20
Speed (E)	0				0				0				0				0			
Endurance	10				10				10				10				10			
Race/Pace	0				0				0				0				0			
Intervals	0				0				0				0				5			
Overdistance	70				70				70				65				60			
Up/Vertical	0				0				0				5				10			
Strength	20				20				20				15				15			

[3] Actual hrs/cycle

[4] Hours per week

	1	2	3	4	5	6	7	8	9	10	11	12	13	14	15	16	17	18	19	20
Actual week number	1	2	3	4	5	6	7	8	9	10	11	12	13	14	15	16	17	18	19	20
Periodization (%) (F)	23	26	29	22	23	26	29	22	23	26	29	22	23	26	29	22	22	27	33	18
Actual hrs/week (G)																				

[5]

Speed (H)																				
Endurance																				
Race/Pace																				
Intervals																				
Overdistance																				
Up/Vertical																				
Strength																				

WORKSHEET B.3, continued

	Four-week cycle	**6**				**7**				**8**				**9**			
	Training stage	INTENSITY				INTENSITY				INTENSITY				PEAK			
	Week numbers	**21 - 24**				**25 - 28**				**29 - 32**				**33 - 36**			
2	**Actual dates (B)**																
	% of year hours (C)	9				9.5				10				8			
3	**Actual hrs/cycle (D)**																
Percent per cycle	**Speed (E)**	5				5				5				5			
Percent per cycle	**Endurance**	5				5				5				5			
Percent per cycle	**Race/Pace**	5				5				5				5			
Percent per cycle	**Intervals**	10				10				10				10			
Percent per cycle	**Overdistance**	60				60				60				60			
Percent per cycle	**Up/Vertical**	5				5				5				5			
Percent per cycle	**Strength**	10				10				10				10			
	Actual week number	**21**	**22**	**23**	**24**	**25**	**26**	**27**	**28**	**29**	**30**	**31**	**32**	**33**	**34**	**35**	**36**
	Periodization (%) (F)	22	27	33	18	22	27	33	18	22	27	33	18	22	27	33	18
4	**Actual hrs/week (G)**																
5 Hours per week	**Speed (H)**																
Hours per week	**Endurance**																
Hours per week	**Race/Pace**																
Hours per week	**Intervals**																
Hours per week	**Overdistance**																
Hours per week	**Up/Vertical**																
Hours per week	**Strength**																

(cont.)

WORKSHEET B.3, continued

	10				11				12				13			
Four-week cycle	10				11				12				13			
Training stage	RACE				RACE				RACE				RESTORATION			
Week numbers	37 - 40				41 - 44				45 - 48				49 - 52			
[2] Actual dates (B)																
% of year hours (C)	7				7				6.5				5			
[3] Actual hrs/cycle (D)																
Speed (E)	10				10				10				0			
Endurance	5				5				5				40			
Race/Pace	15				15				15				0			
Intervals	15				10				10				0			
Overdistance	50				55				55				60			
Up/Vertical	0				0				0				0			
Strength	5				5				5				0			
Actual week number	37	38	39	40	41	42	43	44	45	46	47	48	49	50	51	52
[4] Periodization (%) (F)	30	20	30	20	30	20	30	20	30	20	30	20	25	25	25	25
Actual hrs/week (G)																
[5] Speed (H)																
Endurance																
Race/Pace																
Intervals																
Overdistance																
Up/Vertical																
Strength																

Percent per cycle

Hours per week

WORKSHEET B.4: Marathon, One Competitive Season per Year

Training plan for the year 19___ Name ______________ **1** Projected year hours to train (A) ____

Four-week cycle	1	2	3	4	5
Training stage	BASE	BASE	BASE	BASE	INTENSITY
Week numbers	1 - 4	5 - 8	9 - 12	13 - 16	17 - 20
2 Actual dates (B)					
% of year hours (C)	6	7	8	9	9
3 Actual hrs/cycle (D)					
Percent per cycle					
Speed (E)	0	0	0	0	5
Endurance	10	10	5	10	5
Race/Pace	0	0	0	0	0
Intervals	0	0	0	5	5
Overdistance	70	70	70	65	60
Up/Vertical	0	0	5	5	10
Strength	20	20	20	15	15

Actual week number	1	2	3	4	5	6	7	8	9	10	11	12	13	14	15	16	17	18	19	20
Periodization (%) (F)	23	26	29	22	23	26	29	22	23	26	29	22	23	26	29	22	22	27	33	18
4 Actual hrs/week (G)																				
Hours per week																				
5 Speed (H)																				
Endurance																				
Race/Pace																				
Intervals																				
Overdistance																				
Up/Vertical																				
Strength																				

(cont.)

WORKSHEET B.4, continued

	Four-week cycle	6				7				8				9			
	Training stage	INTENSITY				INTENSITY				INTENSITY				PEAK			
	Week numbers	21 - 24				25 - 28				29 - 32				33 - 36			
2	Actual dates (B)																
	% of year hours (C)	10				11				9				8			
3	Actual hrs/cycle (D)																
	Speed (E)	5				5				5				10			
	Endurance	5				5				5				10			
	Race/Pace	5				5				5				10			
	Intervals	8				10				10				15			
	Overdistance	60				60				60				50			
	Up/Vertical	7				5				5				0			
	Strength	10				10				10				5			
	Actual week number	21	22	23	24	25	26	27	28	29	30	31	32	33	34	35	36
	Periodization (%) (F)	22	27	33	18	22	27	33	18	22	27	33	18	22	27	33	18
4	Actual hrs/week (G)																
5	Speed (H)																
	Endurance																
	Race/Pace																
	Intervals																
	Overdistance																
	Up/Vertical																
	Strength																

Percent per cycle

Hours per week

WORKSHEET B.4, continued

Four-week cycle	10				11				12				13			
Training stage	RACE				RACE				RACE				RESTORATION			
Week numbers	37 - 40				41 - 44				45 - 48				49 - 52			
Actual dates (B)																
% of year hours (C)	7				7				6				3			
Actual hrs/cycle (D)																
Speed (E)	10				10				10				0			
Endurance	5				5				5				40			
Race/Pace	15				15				15				0			
Intervals	15				10				10				0			
Overdistance	50				55				55				60			
Up/Vertical	0				0				0				0			
Strength	5				5				5				0			
Actual week number	37	38	39	40	41	42	43	44	45	46	47	48	49	50	51	52
Periodization (%) (F)	30	20	30	20	30	20	30	20	30	20	30	20	25	25	25	25
Actual hrs/week (G)																
Speed (H)																
Endurance																
Race/Pace																
Intervals																
Overdistance																
Up/Vertical																
Strength																

2 Percent per cycle

3

4 Hours per week

5

WORKSHEET B.5: Cycling—Criteriums, Short Road Races, Time Trials; One Competitive Season per Year

Training plan for the year 19____   Name ____   **1** Projected year hours to train (A) ____

	1	2	3	4	5
Four-week cycle	1	2	3	4	5
Training stage	BASE	BASE	BASE	BASE	INTENSITY
Week numbers	1 - 4	5 - 8	9 - 12	13 - 16	17 - 20
2 Actual dates (B)					
% of year hours (C)	7	7	7.5	8	8.5
3 Actual hrs/cycle (D)					
Speed (E)	0	0	0	0	0
Endurance	10	10	10	10	10
Race/Pace	0	0	0	0	0
Intervals	0	0	0	5	5
Overdistance	70	70	70	65	60
Up/Vertical	0	0	0	5	10
Strength	20	20	20	15	15

(Percent per cycle applies to rows Speed (E) through Strength)

Actual week number	1	2	3	4	5	6	7	8	9	10	11	12	13	14	15	16	17	18	19	20
4 Periodization (%) (F)	23	26	29	22	23	26	29	22	23	26	29	22	23	26	29	22	22	27	33	18
Actual hrs/week (G)																				
5 Speed (H)																				
Endurance																				
Race/Pace																				
Intervals																				
Overdistance																				
Up/Vertical																				
Strength																				

(Hours per week applies to rows Speed (H) through Strength)

WORKSHEET B.5, continued

	Four-week cycle	6				7				8				9			
	Training stage	INTENSITY				INTENSITY				INTENSITY				PEAK			
	Week numbers	**21 - 24**				**25 - 28**				**29 - 32**				**33 - 36**			
2	Actual dates (B)																
	% of year hours (C)	9				9.5				10				8			
3	Actual hrs/cycle (D)																
Percent per cycle	Speed (E)	5				5				5				10			
Percent per cycle	Endurance	5				5				5				10			
Percent per cycle	Race/Pace	5				5				5				10			
Percent per cycle	Intervals	10				10				10				15			
Percent per cycle	Overdistance	60				60				60				50			
Percent per cycle	Up/Vertical	5				5				5				0			
Percent per cycle	Strength	10				10				10				5			
	Actual week number	**21**	**22**	**23**	**24**	**25**	**26**	**27**	**28**	**29**	**30**	**31**	**32**	**33**	**34**	**35**	**36**
	Periodization (%) (F)	22	27	33	18	22	27	33	18	22	27	33	18	22	27	33	18
4	Actual hrs/week (G)																
5 Hours per week	Speed (H)																
Hours per week	Endurance																
Hours per week	Race/Pace																
Hours per week	Intervals																
Hours per week	Overdistance																
Hours per week	Up/Vertical																
Hours per week	Strength																

(cont.)

WORKSHEET B.5, continued

	Four-week cycle	10				11				12				13			
	Training stage	RACE				RACE				RACE				RESTORATION			
	Week numbers	37 - 40				41 - 44				45 - 48				49 - 52			
2	Actual dates (B)																
	% of year hours (C)	7				7				6.5				5			
3	Actual hrs/cycle (D)																
Percent per cycle	Speed (E)	10				10				10				0			
	Endurance	5				5				5				40			
	Race/Pace	15				15				15				0			
	Intervals	15				10				10				0			
	Overdistance	50				55				55				60			
	Up/Vertical	0				0				0				0			
	Strength	5				5				5				0			
	Actual week number	37	38	39	40	41	42	43	44	45	46	47	48	49	50	51	52
4	Periodization (%) (F)	30	20	30	20	30	20	30	20	30	20	30	20	25	25	25	25
5	Actual hrs/week (G)																
Hours per week	Speed (H)																
	Endurance																
	Race/Pace																
	Intervals																
	Overdistance																
	Up/Vertical																
	Strength																

WORKSHEET B.6: Cycling—Longer Road Races, One Competitive Season per Year

Training plan for the year 19 _____   Name _____   **[1]** Projected year hours to train (A) _____

Percent per cycle

		1	2	3	4	5
	Four-week cycle	1	2	3	4	5
	Training stage	BASE	BASE	BASE	BASE	INTENSITY
	Week numbers	1 - 4	5 - 8	9 - 12	13 - 16	17 - 20
[2]	Actual dates (B)					
	% of year hours (C)	6	7	8	9	9
[3]	Actual hrs/cycle (D)					
	Speed (E)	0	0	0	0	5
	Endurance	10	10	5	10	5
	Race/Pace	0	0	0	0	0
	Intervals	0	0	0	5	5
	Overdistance	70	70	70	65	60
	Up/Vertical	0	0	5	5	10
	Strength	20	20	20	15	15

Hours per week

	Actual week number	1	2	3	4	5	6	7	8	9	10	11	12	13	14	15	16	17	18	19	20
[4]	Periodization (%) (F)	23	26	29	22	23	26	29	22	23	26	29	22	23	26	29	22	22	27	33	18
[5]	Actual hrs/week (G)																				
	Speed (H)																				
	Endurance																				
	Race/Pace																				
	Intervals																				
	Overdistance																				
	Up/Vertical																				
	Strength																				

(cont.)

WORKSHEET B.6, continued

		Four-week cycle	6				7				8				9			
		Training stage	INTENSITY				INTENSITY				INTENSITY				PEAK			
		Week numbers	21 - 24				25 - 28				29 - 32				33 - 36			
	2	Actual dates (B)																
		% of year hours (C)	10				11				9				8			
	3	Actual hrs/cycle (D)																
Percent per cycle		Speed (E)	5				5				5				10			
Percent per cycle		Endurance	5				5				5				10			
Percent per cycle		Race/Pace	5				5				5				10			
Percent per cycle		Intervals	8				10				10				15			
Percent per cycle		Overdistance	60				60				60				50			
Percent per cycle		Up/Vertical	7				5				5				0			
Percent per cycle		Strength	10				10				10				5			
		Actual week number	21	22	23	24	25	26	27	28	29	30	31	32	33	34	35	36
		Periodization (%) (F)	22	27	33	18	22	27	33	18	22	27	33	18	22	27	33	18
	4	Actual hrs/week (G)																
Hours per week	5	Speed (H)																
Hours per week		Endurance																
Hours per week		Race/Pace																
Hours per week		Intervals																
Hours per week		Overdistance																
Hours per week		Up/Vertical																
Hours per week		Strength																

WORKSHEET B.6, continued

Four-week cycle	10	11	12	13
Training stage	RACE	RACE	RACE	RESTORATION
Week numbers	37 - 40	41 - 44	45 - 48	49 - 52
2 % of year hours (C)	7	7	6	3
3 Actual hrs/cycle (D)				
Percent per cycle Speed (E)	10	10	10	0
Endurance	5	5	5	40
Race/Pace	15	15	15	0
Intervals	15	10	10	0
Overdistance	50	55	55	60
Up/Vertical	0	0	0	0
Strength	5	5	5	0

	37	38	39	40	41	42	43	44	45	46	47	48	49	50	51	52
Actual week number	37	38	39	40	41	42	43	44	45	46	47	48	49	50	51	52
4 Periodization (%) (F)	30	20	30	20	30	20	30	20	30	20	30	20	25	25	25	25
Actual hrs/week (G)																
5 *Hours per week* Speed (H)																
Endurance																
Race/Pace																
Intervals																
Overdistance																
Up/Vertical																
Strength																

WORKSHEET B.7: Cross-Country Skiing—5 - 25 km, One Competitive Season per Year

Training plan for the year 19_____   Name _____   **[1]** Projected year hours to train (A) _____

Four-week cycle	1	2	3	4	5
Training stage	BASE	BASE	BASE	BASE	INTENSITY
Week numbers	1 - 4	5 - 8	9 - 12	13 - 16	17 - 20
[2] Actual dates (B)					
% of year hours (C)	7	7	7.5	8	8.5
[3] Actual hrs/cycle (D)					

Percent per cycle

	1	2	3	4	5
Speed (E)	0	0	0	0	0
Endurance	10	10	10	10	10
Race/Pace	0	0	0	0	0
Intervals	0	0	0	5	5
Overdistance	70	70	70	65	60
Up/Vertical	0	0	0	5	10
Strength	20	20	20	15	15

Actual week number	1	2	3	4	5	6	7	8	9	10	11	12	13	14	15	16	17	18	19	20
Periodization (%) (F)	23	26	29	22	23	26	29	22	23	26	29	22	23	26	29	22	22	27	33	18
[4] Actual hrs/week (G)																				

[5] **Hours per week**

	1	2	3	4	5	6	7	8	9	10	11	12	13	14	15	16	17	18	19	20
Speed (H)																				
Endurance																				
Race/Pace																				
Intervals																				
Overdistance																				
Up/Vertical																				
Strength																				

WORKSHEET B.7, continued

	21	22	23	24	25	26	27	28	29	30	31	32	33	34	35	36
Four-week cycle	6				7				8				9			
Training stage	INTENSITY				INTENSITY				INTENSITY				PEAK			
Week numbers	21 - 24				25 - 28				29 - 32				33 - 36			
Actual dates (B)																
% of year hours (C)	9				9.5				10				8			
Actual hrs/cycle (D)																
Speed (E)	5				5				5				10			
Endurance	5				5				5				10			
Race/Pace	5				5				5				10			
Intervals	10				10				10				15			
Overdistance	60				60				60				50			
Up/Vertical	5				5				5				0			
Strength	10				10				10				5			
Actual week number	21	22	23	24	25	26	27	28	29	30	31	32	33	34	35	36
Periodization (%) (F)	22	27	33	18	22	27	33	18	22	27	33	18	22	27	33	18
Actual hrs/week (G)																
Speed (H)																
Endurance																
Race/Pace																
Intervals																
Overdistance																
Up/Vertical																
Strength																

Side labels: **2** Actual dates (B); **3** Actual hrs/cycle (D) — *Percent per cycle*; **4** Periodization (%) (F); **5** Actual hrs/week (G) — *Hours per week*

(cont.)

WORKSHEET B.7, continued

	Four-week cycle	10				11				12				13			
	Training stage	RACE				RACE				RACE				RESTORATION			
	Week numbers	37 - 40				41 - 44				45 - 48				49 - 52			
2	Actual dates (B)																
	% of year hours (C)	7				7				6.5				5			
3	Actual hrs/cycle (D)																
Percent per cycle	Speed (E)	10				10				10				0			
	Endurance	5				5				5				40			
	Race/Pace	15				15				15				0			
	Intervals	15				10				10				0			
	Overdistance	50				55				55				60			
	Up/Vertical	0				0				0				0			
	Strength	5				5				5				0			
	Actual week number	37	38	39	40	41	42	43	44	45	46	47	48	49	50	51	52
4	Periodization (%) (F)	30	20	30	20	30	20	30	20	30	20	30	20	25	25	25	25
5	Actual hrs/week (G)																
Hours per week	Speed (H)																
	Endurance																
	Race/Pace																
	Intervals																
	Overdistance																
	Up/Vertical																
	Strength																

WORKSHEET B.8: Cross-Country Skiing—25 - 50 km, One Competitive Season per Year

Training plan for the year 19____   Name _____   **1** Projected year hours to train (A) ____

		1	2	3	4	5
	Four-week cycle	1	2	3	4	5
	Training stage	BASE	BASE	BASE	BASE	INTENSITY
	Week numbers	1 - 4	5 - 8	9 - 12	13 - 16	17 - 20
2	Actual dates (B)					
	% of year hours (C)	6	7	8	9	9
3	Actual hrs/cycle (D)					
Percent per cycle	Speed (E)	0	0	0	0	5
	Endurance	10	10	5	10	5
	Race/Pace	0	0	0	0	0
	Intervals	0	0	0	5	5
	Overdistance	70	70	70	65	60
	Up/Vertical	0	0	5	5	10
	Strength	20	20	20	15	15

	1	2	3	4	5	6	7	8	9	10	11	12	13	14	15	16	17	18	19	20
Actual week number	1	2	3	4	5	6	7	8	9	10	11	12	13	14	15	16	17	18	19	20
4 Periodization (%) (F)	23	26	29	22	23	26	29	22	23	26	29	22	23	26	29	22	22	27	33	18
5 Actual hrs/week (G)																				
Speed (H)																				
Endurance																				
Race/Pace																				
Intervals																				
Overdistance																				
Up/Vertical																				
Strength																				

(Hours per week)

(cont.)

WORKSHEET B.8, continued

		6				7				8				9			
	Four-week cycle																
	Training stage	INTENSITY				INTENSITY				INTENSITY				PEAK			
	Week numbers	21 - 24				25 - 28				29 - 32				33 - 36			
[2]	Actual dates (B)																
	% of year hours (C)	10				11				9				8			
[3]	Actual hrs/cycle (D)																
Percent per cycle	Speed (E)	5				5				5				10			
	Endurance	5				5				5				10			
	Race/Pace	5				5				5				10			
	Intervals	8				10				10				15			
	Overdistance	60				60				60				50			
	Up/Vertical	7				5				5				0			
	Strength	10				10				10				5			
	Actual week number	21	22	23	24	25	26	27	28	29	30	31	32	33	34	35	36
[4]	Periodization (%) (F)	22	27	33	18	22	27	33	18	22	27	33	18	22	27	33	18
	Actual hrs/week (G)																
[5] Hours per week	Speed (H)																
	Endurance																
	Race/Pace																
	Intervals																
	Overdistance																
	Up/Vertical																
	Strength																

WORKSHEET B.8, continued

Four-week cycle	10	11	12	13
Training stage	RACE	RACE	RACE	RESTORATION
Week numbers	37 - 40	41 - 44	45 - 48	49 - 52
[2] Actual dates (B)				
% of year hours (C)	7	7	6	3
[3] Actual hrs/cycle (D)				
Percent per cycle: Speed (E)	10	10	10	0
Endurance	5	5	5	40
Race/Pace	15	15	15	0
Intervals	15	10	10	0
Overdistance	50	55	55	60
Up/Vertical	0	0	0	0
Strength	5	5	5	0

Actual week number	37	38	39	40	41	42	43	44	45	46	47	48	49	50	51	52
[4] Periodization (%) (F)	30	20	30	20	30	20	30	20	30	20	30	20	25	25	25	25
Actual hrs/week (G)																
[5] *Hours per week:* Speed (H)																
Endurance																
Race/Pace																
Intervals																
Overdistance																
Up/Vertical																
Strength																

WORKSHEET B.9: Two Competitive Seasons per Year—Cross-Country Skiing, 10 - 50 km, Weeks 1 - 24; Triathlon, USTS to Ironman Distances, Weeks 25 - 52

Training plan for the year 19____   Name _____   **1** Projected year hours to train (A) ____

Four-week cycle	1	2	3	4	5
Training stage	BASE	BASE	INTENSITY	INTENSITY	RACE 1
Week numbers	1 - 4	5 - 8	9 - 12	13 - 16	17 - 20
2 Actual dates (B)					
% of year hours (C)	7.5	7.5	8.5	9	7.5
3 Actual hrs/cycle (D)					

Percent per cycle

	1	2	3	4	5
Speed (E)	0	0	5	5	10
Endurance	10	10	10	10	10
Race/Pace	0	0	0	5	5
Intervals	0	0	5	10	10
Overdistance	70	65	60	60	55
Up/Vertical	5	10	10	0	0
Strength	15	15	10	10	5

Hours per week

Actual week number	1	2	3	4	5	6	7	8	9	10	11	12	13	14	15	16	17	18	19	20
Periodization (%) (F)	23	26	29	22	23	26	29	22	22	27	33	18	22	27	33	18	30	20	30	20
4 Actual hrs/week (G)																				
5 Speed (H)																				
Endurance																				
Race/Pace																				
Intervals																				
Overdistance																				
Up/Vertical																				
Strength																				

WORKSHEET B.9, continued

	6	7	8	9
Four-week cycle				
Training stage	RACE 1	REST	BASE	BASE
Week numbers	21 - 24	25 - 28	29 - 32	33 - 36
Actual dates (B)				
% of year hours (C)	7.5	5	7.5	7.5
Actual hrs/cycle (D)				
Speed (E)	10	0	0	0
Endurance	5	40	10	10
Race/Pace	15	0	0	0
Intervals	10	0	0	0
Overdistance	55	60	70	70
Up/Vertical	0	0	5	10
Strength	5	0	15	10

[2] Percent per cycle (rows: % of year hours through Strength)
[3] (Actual hrs/cycle)

Actual week number	21	22	23	24	25	26	27	28	29	30	31	32	33	34	35	36
Periodization (%) (F)	30	20	30	20	25	25	25	25	23	26	29	22	23	26	29	22
Actual hrs/week (G)																
Speed (H)																
Endurance																
Race/Pace																
Intervals																
Overdistance																
Up/Vertical																
Strength																

[4] [5] Hours per week

(cont.)

WORKSHEET B.9, continued

	6				7				8				9			
Four-week cycle	6				7				8				9			
Training stage	RACE 1				REST				BASE				BASE			
Week numbers	21 - 24				25 - 28				29 - 32				33 - 36			
Actual dates (B)																
% of year hours (C)	7.5				5				7.5				7.5			
Actual hrs/cycle (D)																
Speed (E)	10				0				0				0			
Endurance	5				40				10				10			
Race/Pace	15				0				0				0			
Intervals	10				0				0				0			
Overdistance	55				60				70				70			
Up/Vertical	0				0				5				10			
Strength	5				0				15				10			
Actual week number	21	22	23	24	25	26	27	28	29	30	31	32	33	34	35	36
Periodization (%) (F)	30	20	30	20	25	25	25	25	23	26	29	22	23	26	29	22
Actual hrs/week (G)																
Speed (H)																
Endurance																
Race/Pace																
Intervals																
Overdistance																
Up/Vertical																
Strength																

Left-side markers: **2**, **3** (Percent per cycle), **4**, **5** (Hours per week)

(cont.)

WORKSHEET B.9, continued

	10				11				12				13			
Four-week cycle	10				11				12				13			
Training stage	INTENSITY				INTENSITY				RACE 2				RACE 2			
Week numbers	37 - 40				41 - 44				45 - 48				49 - 52			
[2] Actual dates (B)																
[3] % of year hours (C)	8.5				9				7.5				7.5			
Actual hrs/cycle (D)																
Percent per cycle																
Speed (E)	5				5				10				10			
Endurance	10				10				10				10			
Race/Pace	10				10				15				15			
Intervals	5				10				10				10			
Overdistance	60				60				55				55			
Up/Vertical	10				5				0				0			
Strength	0				0				0				0			
Actual week number	37	38	39	40	41	42	43	44	45	46	47	48	49	50	51	52
[4] Periodization (%) (F)	30	20	30	20	30	20	30	20	30	20	30	20	25	25	25	25
Actual hrs/week (G)																
Hours per week																
[5] Speed (H)																
Endurance																
Race/Pace																
Intervals																
Overdistance																
Up/Vertical																
Strength																

WORKSHEET B.10: Two Competitive Seasons per Year—Cross-Country Skiing, 10 - 50 km, Weeks 1 - 24; Cycling, Road Races, Weeks 25 - 52

Training plan for the year 19 ____   Name ____   [1] Projected year hours to train (A) ____

Percent per cycle [2] [3]

Four-week cycle	1	2	3	4	5
Training stage	BASE	BASE	INTENSITY	INTENSITY	RACE 1
Week numbers	1 - 4	5 - 8	9 - 12	13 - 16	17 - 20
Actual dates (B)					
% of year hours (C)	7.5	7.5	8.5	9	7.5
Actual hrs/cycle (D)					
Speed (E)	0	0	5	5	10
Endurance	10	10	5	10	5
Race/Pace	0	0	0	5	15
Intervals	0	0	5	10	10
Overdistance	70	65	60	60	55
Up/Vertical	5	10	10	0	0
Strength	15	15	10	10	5

Hours per week [4] [5]

Actual week number	1	2	3	4	5	6	7	8	9	10	11	12	13	14	15	16	17	18	19	20
Periodization (%) (F)	23	26	29	22	23	26	29	22	22	27	33	18	22	27	33	18	30	20	30	20
Actual hrs/week (G)																				
Speed (H)																				
Endurance																				
Race/Pace																				
Intervals																				
Overdistance																				
Up/Vertical																				
Strength																				

(cont.)

WORKSHEET B.10, continued

	6				7				8				9			
Four-week cycle																
Training stage	RACE 1				REST				BASE				BASE			
Week numbers	21 - 24				25 - 28				29 - 32				33 - 36			
Actual dates (B)																
% of year hours (C)	7.5				5				7.5				7.5			
Actual hrs/cycle (D)																
Percent per cycle																
Speed (E)	10				0				0				0			
Endurance	5				40				10				10			
Race/Pace	15				0				0				0			
Intervals	10				0				0				0			
Overdistance	55				60				70				70			
Up/Vertical	0				0				5				10			
Strength	5				0				15				10			
Actual week number	21	22	23	24	25	26	27	28	29	30	31	32	33	34	35	36
Periodization (%) (F)	30	20	30	20	25	25	25	25	23	26	29	22	23	26	29	22
Actual hrs/week (G)																
Hours per week																
Speed (H)																
Endurance																
Race/Pace																
Intervals																
Overdistance																
Up/Vertical																
Strength																

WORKSHEET B.10, continued

Four-week cycle	10	11	12	13
Training stage	INTENSITY	INTENSITY	RACE 2	RACE 2
Week numbers	37 - 40	41 - 44	45 - 48	49 - 52
Actual dates (B)				
% of year hours (C)	8.5	9	7.5	7.5
Actual hrs/cycle (D)				
Speed (E)	5	5	10	10
Endurance	10	10	10	10
Race/Pace	10	10	15	15
Intervals	5	10	10	10
Overdistance	60	60	55	55
Up/Vertical	10	5	0	0
Strength	0	0	0	0

(Left-side markers: 2; 3 — Percent per cycle)

Actual week number	37	38	39	40	41	42	43	44	45	46	47	48	49	50	51	52
Periodization (%) (F)	30	20	30	20	30	20	30	20	30	20	30	20	25	25	25	25
Actual hrs/week (G)																
Speed (H)																
Endurance																
Race/Pace																
Intervals																
Overdistance																
Up/Vertical																
Strength																

(Left-side markers: 4; 5 — Hours per week)

WORKSHEET B.11: Two Competitive Seasons per Year—Running, 10 km, Weeks 1 - 24; Running, Marathon, Weeks 25 - 52

Training plan for the year 19____   Name _____   **1** Projected year hours to train (A) _____

	1	2	3	4	5
Four-week cycle	1	2	3	4	5
Training stage	BASE	BASE	INTENSITY	INTENSITY	RACE 1
Week numbers	1 - 4	5 - 8	9 - 12	13 - 16	17 - 20
Actual dates (B)					
% of year hours (C)	7.5	7.5	8.5	9	7.5
Actual hrs/cycle (D)					
Speed (E)	0	0	5	5	10
Endurance	10	10	10	10	10
Race/Pace	0	0	0	5	15
Intervals	0	0	5	10	10
Overdistance	70	70	60	60	55
Up/Vertical	5	10	10	0	0
Strength	15	10	10	10	0

2 = Actual dates (B); **3** = Actual hrs/cycle (D); *Percent per cycle*

Actual week number	1	2	3	4	5	6	7	8	9	10	11	12	13	14	15	16	17	18	19	20
Periodization (%) (F)	23	26	29	22	23	26	29	22	22	27	33	18	22	27	33	18	30	20	30	20
Actual hrs/week (G)																				
Speed (H)																				
Endurance																				
Race/Pace																				
Intervals																				
Overdistance																				
Up/Vertical																				
Strength																				

4 = Actual hrs/week (G); **5** = Speed (H); *Hours per week*

WORKSHEET B.11, continued

Four-week cycle	6	7	8	9
Training stage	RACE 1	REST	BASE	BASE:
Week numbers	21 - 24	25 - 28	29 - 32	33 - 36
2 Actual dates (B)				
3 % of year hours (C)	7.5	5	7.5	7.5
Actual hrs/cycle (D)				
Speed (E)	10	0	0	0
Endurance	10	40	10	10
Race/Pace	15	0	0	0
Intervals	10	0	0	0
Overdistance	55	60	70	70
Up/Vertical	0	0	10	10
Strength	0	0	10	10

(Percent per cycle)

Actual week number	21	22	23	24	25	26	27	28	29	30	31	32	33	34	35	36
4 Periodization (%) (F)	30	20	30	20	25	25	25	25	23	26	29	22	23	26	29	22
5 Actual hrs/week (G)																
Speed (H)																
Endurance																
Race/Pace																
Intervals																
Overdistance																
Up/Vertical																
Strength																

(Hours per week)

(cont.)

WORKSHEET B.11, continued

Four-week cycle	10				11				12				13			
Training stage	INTENSITY				INTENSITY				RACE 2				RACE 2			
Week numbers	37 - 40				41 - 44				45 - 48				49 - 52			
Actual dates (B)																
% of year hours (C)	8.5				9				7.5				7.5			
Actual hrs/cycle (D)																
Percent per cycle — Speed (E)	5				5				10				10			
Endurance	10				10				10				10			
Race/Pace	0				5				10				10			
Intervals	10				10				10				10			
Overdistance	65				65				60				60			
Up/Vertical	5				0				0				0			
Strength	5				5				0				0			
Actual week number	37	38	39	40	41	42	43	44	45	46	47	48	49	50	51	52
Periodization (%) (F)	22	27	33	18	22	27	33	18	30	20	30	20	30	20	30	20
Hours per week — Actual hrs/week (G)																
Speed (H)																
Endurance																
Race/Pace																
Intervals																
Overdistance																
Up/Vertical																
Strength																

HOW TO DO SERIOUS WORKOUTS FOR ENDURANCE SPORTS

There are many ways to accomplish specific training components. Translating the SERIOUS system into the training language you may have been using will be straightforward. In fact, you'll probably be able to easily tailor the personality of each SERIOUS workout to fit your experiences and needs. You can mix and match from your repertoire of training techniques to sculpt your own workouts, if you desire. Workout time allotment and intensity are the critical factors for each training component. As long as you consider those two factors in planning each component, the relative physiological benefit will be positive.

The following descriptions of every SERIOUS component outline the benefits, methods, and types of workouts used to accomplish each component. The descriptions are based on the current thinking of physiologists, coaches, and trainers regarding training for peak fitness. Use them in conjunction with your personal experience. This is not a complete guide. There are many available sources that you may want to use to increase your training effectiveness.

Speed Training

Benefit

Speed workouts train the neuromuscular system to coordinate rapid muscle firing at rates above race speed. The primary goal is to improve coordination and flexibility. The anaerobic energy pathways and capacity of the fast-twitch muscle fibers are also increased. The key to Speed training, regardless of the activity used, is the ease with which the workouts are accomplished. It is essential that you learn to *release* your speed, rather than force it with powerful movements. You must maintain economy of movement, performing each Speed session with light, easy, yet fast motion. Search for the fastest use of your muscles with the least energy expended.

Method of Activity

It is best to do Speed sessions using the activity you compete in. CAUTION: To prevent injury, do not use Speed work in running unless you have a strong running base or are running about 20 miles per week.

Types of Speed Workouts

1. Tempo Speed Bursts

These are very brief speed releases used only during Overdistance workouts. Every 10 to 15 minutes during OD sessions, gradually increase your speed until it is about 10% to 20% faster than your fastest race speed. The buildup to this speed should take about 10 seconds. Once it is attained, hold that speed for 6 to 10 seconds maximum. Resume OD workout pace. IMPORTANT: Concentrate on ease of movement. Your intensity must remain aerobic. Let the muscles stay relaxed—this is when the learning takes place. These are not hard sprints.

2. Body Speeds

These are done as specific workouts. After a 20- to 40-minute warm-up, select a section of track (or road) that is 200 meters in length (if you are cycling, choose a 600- to 800-meter section). Gradually increase your speed during the section, concentrating on releasing the speed and removing tension. You should feel a floating sensation. At the end of the section, slow down and continue to move easily until your heart rate reaches 120 bpm. Then start the next section. Repeat until your allotted time is up for that session. Finish with a 20-minute active cool-down.

   Increase your Body Speeds by decreasing your time per 200-meter section by 1 to 2 seconds every 2 to 3 weeks. You should be able to do the 200-meter section at a pace 5 to 10 seconds per kilometer faster than your race pace by the time your first race arrives. For example, if I want to race this year at a 3 minute per kilometer pace, I should be doing my Body Speeds at 34 seconds per 200 meters, which is a 2:50 minute per kilometer pace, by the time my first race arrives.

To determine 200-meter Body Speeds pace:

   Using Tables C.1 and C.2, choose a pace per kilometer that you realistically feel you can race this season. Subtract 10 seconds from this time to arrive at the Body Speed adjusted pace. Now choose the time for 200 meters at that pace. Add 1 or 2 seconds to this time every 2 or 3 weeks until you reach the beginning of speed workouts in your schedule.

Table C.1

Determining Body Speed Pace for Running and Cross-Country Skiing

Race speed (min/km)	Body speed (sec/200m)
2:30	30
2:35	31
2:40	32
2:45	33
2:50	34
2:55	35
3:00	36
3:05	37
3:10	38
3:15	39
3:20	40
3:25	41
3:30	42
3:35	43
3:40	44
3:45	45
3:50	46
3:55	47
4:00	48
4:05	49
4:10	50
4:15	51
4:20	52
4:25	53
4:30	54
4:35	55
4:40	56
4:45	57
4:50	58
4:55	59
5:00	60

Table C.2
Determing Body Speed Pace for Cycling

Race speed mph	Body speed - seconds/distance		
	0.2 miles	0.3 miles	0.4 miles
15.0	48	72	96
15.5	46	70	93
16.0	45	68	90
16.5	44	65	87
17.0	42	64	85
17.5	41	62	82
18.0	40	60	80
18.5	39	58	78
19.0	38	57	76
19.5	37	55	74
20.0	36	54	72
20.5	35	53	70
21.0	34	51	69
21.5	33	50	67
22.0	33	49	65
22.5	32	48	64
23.0	31	47	63
23.5	31	46	61
24.0	30	45	60
24.5	29	44	59
25.0	29	43	58
25.5	28	42	56
26.0	28	42	55
26.5	27	41	54
27.0	27	40	53
27.5	26	39	52
28.0	26	39	51
28.5	25	38	51
29.0	25	37	50
29.5	24	37	49
30.0	24	36	48

3. Peaking Sprints

These are all-out efforts at your fastest speed while maintaining good form. Peaking sprints are used only during the Peak and Racing stages to refine your fast-twitch muscle fiber recruitment and anaerobic energy systems. Accomplish this by releasing the speed without tense, straining movements. Choose average racecourse terrain and complete the scheduled time with repeats of 15-second sprints followed by 15 to 60 seconds of easy recovery. You may find it best to do 3 or 4 sets of five to ten 15-second sprints, with a few minutes' rest between sets. These workouts must be preceded by 20 to 40 minutes of warm-up.

Peaking Sprints should be quite difficult. They are the finishing touches on your training and will help you "ride" a peak for 8 to 12 weeks if you use them during the Racing stage. They should be performed at a Level V intensity (you may need to rate this subjectively as a Level V, rather than use heart rate, because heart rate may not always reach maximum for these workouts).

Table C.3 indicates proper use of SPEED workouts in relation to each training stage of the year.

Table C.3
Speed Work for Various Stages of Training

Stage	Type	Intensity
Base	Tempo speed bursts	Level I
	Body speeds	Level II
Intensity	Tempo speed bursts	Level I
	Body speeds	Level II
Peak	Tempo speed bursts	Level I
	Peaking sprints	Level V
Race	Tempo speed bursts	Level I
	Peaking sprints	Level V

Endurance/Easy Distance Training

Benefit

Endurance workouts are of medium length at low to medium intensity. Endurance workouts are designed to be used as warm-up and cool-down training or to allow variety in the training schedule. These are great for doing a different type of training to break up the routine, check out a new aerobics class, try a mountain bike, or play in a rowing shell. Maybe you'll use these to explore new training areas. Whatever the case, accomplish these at Level II intensity for the designated time on your schedule.

Method of Activity

The closer you come to competition season, the more sport-specific these sessions should be. However, it is all right to try other activities for these sessions. For example, if you are a cross-country skier but do a fair amount of running or cycling for your dryland training, it is a good idea to continue using these activities regularly during the ski season, perhaps once or twice per week. This may help prevent overuse syndromes and injuries when you make the transition from snow to dryland training.

Race/Pace Training

Benefit

Race/Pace workouts are designed to provide both training benefit and learning experiences from actual competition. The key is knowing the difference between racing at maximum effort and Race/Pacing at current fitness levels.

Method of Activity

It's ideal to accomplish these sessions using the sport you will eventually compete in. However, it's refreshing to use other sports once in awhile.

Types of Race/Pace

1. Timed Trials

A timed trial is a workout in which you perform at the specified intensity (ideally using a heart monitor that has memory capability for recording the entire workout) and time, while recording the distance. The essence of these sessions is the discipline required to maintain prescribed intensity and duration. Perform these with an attitude of control and low stress, concentrating on moving smoothly and with regard to your body's inner language. I suggest that you use the same measured course every other week at most, and on the other weeks use a different course where you will focus on your feelings rather than on distance performance. Because your schedule dictates the time length of these trials (because of the calculation of Year Hours), you must take a set time in which to accomplish the measured distance.

Improvement in time over a given distance every single week is not the most important aspect of timed trials. Rather, improving efficiency, control, and pace are of greater significance, and these can be practiced on the off weeks when you do the Pace workout simply for the time allotment on your schedule.

CAUTION: Race/Pace workouts performed at maximal effort during early stages of training will merely offer a quick fix of instant gratification and will detract from reaching a planned peak, if one is reached at all. Level IV intensity is the maximum allowed for timed trials. Try to stay in control and keep intensity below your AT pace.

2. Racing

The advent of the Peak stage and Racing stage brings true racing efforts. Here you may perform your races with personal bests in mind. The training program you have followed to date has prepared you to unleash your best. Now is the time to go for it, listening to your body's signals along the way. Level IV and V intensities will be reached during racing.

Again, during racing season you may want to adjust your schedule so that you are racing only once or twice per 4-week cycle. This will depend on how long the races in which you plan to participate are. You can adjust the total 4-week cycle Race/Pace time allotment to meet your needs.

Interval Training

Benefit

Interval training challenges the body to carry and deliver oxygen to the working muscle cells for short periods of relatively intense work before too much lactic acid builds up. Fast-twitch and slow-twitch fibers are recruited during intervals, encouraging improvement in their oxidative capabilities.

Method of Activity

The closer you are to the Racing stage, the more sport-specific you need to be in doing Intervals. However, early in the season they can be done effectively with other sports, using caution to avoid injury.

Types of Intervals

It's a good idea to alternate types from week to week.

1. Fartlek

Often called *speed play*, Fartlek is a continuous session lasting the time allotted on your schedule for Interval work. Intervals of faster movement occur virtually whenever and wherever you like—on the flats, up hills, and down hills. It is important to learn to go fast on every type of terrain. Choose interesting and varying terrain on which to do Fartlek.

There are some rules to Fartlek. The length of the intervals must be increased gradually throughout the year, beginning with efforts of not more than 1 minute and ending with lengths up to 10 minutes by the Peak Stage. Increase the length of each interval by about 30 seconds every 1 or 2 weeks. Each effort must be followed by enough active recovery time to allow the heart rate to drop to 130 bpm. Speed play implies unsystematic, spontaneous effort designed to allow you to tune in to your rhythm and speed. Relax and enjoy this type of interval training. The level of intensity must not exceed Level IV. Always warm up for 20 minutes before Fartlek.

2. Flat Repeat Intervals

These intervals involve the use of a smooth section of ski track, a running track, a section of flat road, or the pool. As with Fartlek, it is important to increase the length of each interval gradually and systematically every 1 or 2 weeks by about 30 seconds until the length of each has reached 6 to 10 minutes. Recover until your heart rate drops below 130 bpm. This type of interval allows you to time a given distance at the prescribed level of intensity, Level IV, thus making it easier to check your progress and level of conditioning. Always warm up for 20 minutes beforehand.

CAUTION: With all Intervals, strict attention must be made to maintaining a Level IV intensity, slightly below the anaerobic threshold. Your arms and legs should not feel spent or rubbery during or after Intervals. If they do, you have trained too hard and you must stop the workout and cool down. Form and technique are very important during Intervals. If either breaks down during the session, that may be the cue to end the workout. A heart monitor is a great tool for Intervals.

Overdistance Training

Benefit

OD training brings increased capillary density, improved ability to mobilize and use fatty acids as fuel, increased mitochondria numbers and efficiency, and increased levels of oxidative enzymes in cells. Overdistance serves as the foundation for all other training. It prepares the body for higher intensity work in other components of SERIOUS training. Overdistance training serves as excellent training for working on technique and form as well.

Method of Activity

I recommend that you use a variety of activities to accomplish these workouts. Skiing, hiking, running, cycling, rowing and swimming alone or in combination in one workout will bring about a good conditioning effect. Once again, the closer you get to racing season, the more sport-specific you need to be.

Type of Overdistance

The most important factor for OD work is the amount of time spent working at the lowest level of intensity, Level I. Your training schedule has outlined this for you. Physiologically, your body will adapt to the long distance. Psychologically, you'll become disciplined, tough, and confident that you can go the distance. Use the OD workouts as easy, comfortable, and enjoyable exercise. You'll be tired enough by the end of the session. Overdistance can be considered high-stress exercise. The natural tendency will be to think that it is too easy. Pay close attention to the intensity. Do not exceed Level I for these workouts. OD training should be done at a "guilt-producingly-easy" intensity. Heart monitors are highly recommended for these workouts because they help you maintain the correct intensity.

Up/Vertical or Hill Interval Training

Benefit

Vertical training is the same as Interval training except that you do the workouts up hills or against considerable resistance, such as a headwind. Vertical training should be at a Level IV intensity—just below the anaerobic threshold, which produces that burning-legs-and-lungs feeling. The aerobic power developed during Vertical training occurs in the muscle fibers recruited to move your body against gravity. Theoretically, they do one-third of the work in a race.

Method of Training

Accomplish these workouts in a sport-specific manner, if possible. Vary the steepness of your hills to recruit a wide variety of fibers. If you do not have hills to train on, try finding a prevailing headwind for the added resistance.

Types of Vertical Training

Alternate types every week.

1. General Vertical

Using moderately steep terrain, accomplish these intervals at Level IV intensity, paying close attention to form and technique in order to find the most efficient ways of climbing. Increase the length of these Verticals from 1 minute at the beginning of Vertical training to 6 minutes by the end of Vertical training. Always recover until your pulse is below 130 bpm before beginning the next interval. Warm up for at least 20 minutes for this session.

2. Sprittsprunge (a West German biathlon team favorite)

This is hill bounding, using extremely steep terrain. Accomplish these very difficult intervals at Level IV intensity by bounding up the slope, exaggerating the springing motion by striding out as far as possible. These intervals are 1 minute in duration, with recovery until pulse is below 130 bpm. Repeat until allotted time is up. Warm up for at least 20 minutes beforehand.

3. Fartlek

Accomplished in the same manner as Fartlek Intervals except that you push hard on the hills. It is necessary to choose a hilly course.

Strength Training

Strength training is subject to a diversity of opinions and methods regarding proper implementation. Although the following guidelines may give you some ideas for Strength training, it is highly recommended that you consult with knowledgeable sources and reference material before embarking on your Strength program. It's just not possible to provide enough detail in this book regarding the variety of strength-training methods. Use common sense and caution in selecting and devising your own routines.

Benefit

Strength work is necessary to maintain muscle balance and flexibility and to prevent injuries. Particular attention must be given to the abdominal muscles so that the integrity of the lower back muscles and posture are maintained.

Method of Training

Many devices and exercises may be used to develop sport-specific strength. Rollerboards, slideboards, rubber tubing, free weights, Nautilus and Universal weight machines, plyometrics, and calisthenics all work well. Following are a few ways in which you can do Strength workouts.

CAUTION: Always warm up for 10 to 20 minutes before Strength training.

Types of Strength Training

Formulate your own Strength routines using the guidelines below. Three different routines are recommended; these should be alternated as the schedule indicates.

1. Upper-Body Strength

A. Rollerboard (for cross-country skiing).   The best way to use a rollerboard is to position your body so that you are standing, straddling the board or rail with your feet resting on "stirrups." If you cannot build one like this, then sit on your rollerboard cart with your legs dangling from your knees.

There are many variations to the rollerboard workout. You can vary the repetitions per set from 25 to over 100. You can vary the angle of the board to increase or decrease resistance. You can change the height of the attachment for the pull ropes so that your muscles get worked over a greater range of motion. You can also vary the width of the attachment of the pull ropes to work the muscles slightly differently. You can pull with great force, power, and speed, or you can pull with slow, rhythmic strokes. Over the course of the week, it is recommended that you include at least one of each of the following in your rollerboard workouts:

1. Low-angle board, 100 reps with slow pulls, 3- to 5-minute recovery. Repeat.
2. Medium-angle board, 50 reps with higher tempo rhythmic pulls, 2-minute recovery. Repeat.
3. Steep-angle board, 25 reps with fast, powerful strokes, 2-minute recovery. Repeat.

B. Lifeline Gym, Exergenie, rubber tubing.   These devices are versatile, providing exercise for many muscles of the upper body. The same workouts and principles used for rollerboard apply to these devices. You may need to have different "weights" of rubber tubing or Lifeline Gyms to get variable resistance. These are great to have because you can take them with you on trips.

C. Circuit calisthenics.   Complete each exercise in the following circuit for as many repetitions as possible. If it causes strain or hurts, don't push it. Take 30 to 60 seconds of recovery between exercises. Repeat the circuit if time permits. Always work on weak areas first. It's more fun to do the circuit with music. Many athletes make their own music tapes with appropriately timed sequences for exercise and recovery.

1. *Bent-Knee Sit-Ups*. Lie on your back, knees bent, feet flat on the floor, arms crossed over chest, and chin tucked to chest. Sit up on a two count, down on a four count. Do not snap upward or try to gain momentum, or you may hurt your lower back.
2. *Abdominal Crunches*. Same as bent-knee sit-ups except you put your lower legs and feet up on a chair seat.
3. *Pull-Ups*. Grab a bar above your head, palms facing away from you. Pull yourself up on one count, down on two. You can modify this by placing a broomstick across two chair seats and lying under the bar with your body extended; lift yourself up to the bar, leaving your heels on the floor.
4. *Arm Dips*. Use a dip bar if possible. If not, sit between two chairs with legs extended and heels on the floor. Place palms of hands on chair seats to each side. Lift yourself up by extending arms on one count, down on two. Buttocks do not touch floor.
5. *Leg Dips*. Using a chair, stairs, or post about 18 inches high, step up with one foot, fully extending leg on one count, stepping back down on two. Repeat with other leg. Alternate for up to 20 repetitions each side.
6. *Skate Step*. On a soft surface, hop from side to side as if you were skiing or skating, bending your upper body slightly. Do for 30 to 60 seconds.
7. *Phantom Chair (Wall Sit)*. Sit with your back against the wall, with legs in 90-degree angle at the knees. Your legs should support you. Hold as long as possible or do repetitions of 1 minute each. This is good for strengthening the muscles of the upper leg, which provide stability to the knee.

D. Weight Training.   Regardless of whether you use free weights or Nautilus, Universal, or other weight machines, be sure to get proper instruction on using them. Because you are interested in building endurance strength rather than "bulking up," complete each exercise using a weight that allows you to complete 15 to 20 repetitions. Recover for 30 to 60 seconds between sets. Choose the exercises that are most specific for each sport. Do as many sets of the circuit as time allows.

2. Legs

A. Plyometrics.   These are explosive, calisthenic-like jumping exercises used to develop power in the leg muscles. Plyometric routines must be done on very soft surfaces like grass or dirt. Be sure to use supportive, cushioned footwear such as high-top basketball shoes. Increase the number of repetitions very gradually in order to prevent soreness or injury. It is recommended that you establish a good strength-training base before incorporating plyometrics into your program.

1. *Hops*. Hop high into the air and forward up a moderate hill, landing on the hopping foot and then switching to other foot to hop again. Repeat up to 15 times on each leg.
2. *Skate Hops*. Using a skating motion, hop from one foot to the other as you progress over a flat or up a slight hill. Be sure to pause slightly on the landing leg in order to load the muscles for the next hop. Do up to 15 repetitions per leg.
3. *Vertical Jumps (two legs)*. With feet parallel, bend slightly at knees and jump as high as possible, land, load muscles, and jump again. Do up to 15 jumps per set.
4. *Vertical Jumps (one leg at a time)*. This is the same as the previous exercise except you jump with one leg and land on the other.

B. Weights.   Traditional weight lifting can be good for some early-season strength training. Squats, leg presses, leg extensions, leg curls, lunges, and calf raises are all good as long as you use weights that you can lift for 15 to 20 repetitions.

Suggestions for Using More Than One Routine

These guidelines are based on the Strength schedule used by elite athletes whom I coach. You can use these routines to incorporate the various strength circuits for your schedule.

Routine 1

Combination of calisthenics and plyometrics in a circuit fashion. Abdominal exercises should be included. This is a good circuit for which to prepare a music tape for accompaniment.

Routine 2

Weight circuit, using free weights or Nautilus, Universal, or other machines of comparable function. Do the circuit using high repetitions and low weights, 15 to 20 reps at a given weight. Increase weight only when 20 reps are easily lifted.

Routine 3

Sport-specific strength exercises, such as rollerboard, slideboard, double-poling up hills, and Exergenie for cross-country skiers. Determine the sport-specific exercises for your sport and incorporate them into your routine.

SERIOUS *SYSTEM* *TRAINING LOG,* *JOURNAL, AND* *PERFORMANCE* <u>*GRAPH*</u>

Week #___	Day Time	1 A B	2 A B	3 A B	4 A B	5 A B	6 A B	7 A B	Totals
Date									
Speed									
Endurance									
Race/Pace									
Interval									
Overdistance									
Up/Vertical									
Strength									
Intensity (I - V)									
Bicycle									
Hiking									
Rowing									
Ski X-C									
Swimming									
Running									
Other									
Stretching									
Feeling (1 - 5)									
Workout completed? Y/N									
Morning pulse									
Morning weight									
Sleep hours									

Figure D.1 SERIOUS system training log.

Journal

Day/Date	Week of / / Week #

1

2

3

4

5

6

7

Figure D.2 SERIOUS system journal format.

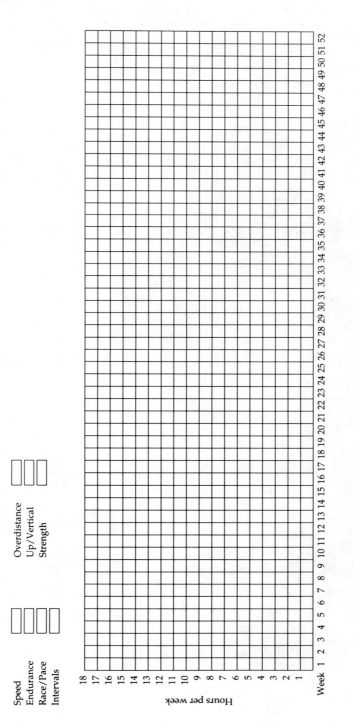

Figure D.3 Format for keeping a yearlong performance graph.

DETERMINING LACTATE THRESHOLD BY NONINVASIVE MEANS

In chapter 5 on Intensity, I mentioned the concept of anaerobic threshold (AT) (synonymous with lactate threshold or LT) training, equal to Level IV on the heart rate intensity scale. AT training, or threshold training, has become a very popular training concept. The scientist who has become perhaps most noted for his techniques for determining the AT is Italian physician and physiologist Francesco Conconi, who developed a method for measuring an endurance athlete's AT by noninvasive means (without taking blood samples).

As described in chapter 5, Level IV intensity training is intended to be synonymous with AT training. It is exercising at or slightly below the intensity that causes changes in ventilation from rhythmic and deep to shallow and erratic; rubbery legs and arms; and the subjective feeling that if you push any harder, you will probably "go under." It is very important that you learn to feel what it is like to be at the AT.

Using threshold training for a certain percentage of your total training volume will stimulate your body to adapt to going at hard intensities. You will increase your $\dot{V}O_2$max. Most importantly, you will increase the percentage of your $\dot{V}O_2$max that you can effectively use before the debilitating effects of lactic acid buildup and burning set in. In other words, you will improve your ability to maintain a fast pace.

For example, one runner I work with did a small experiment in a 10K race. One week prior to the race, we determined his AT to be at a heart rate of 172 bpm, allowing him a running pace that theoretically would have him finish the race in just over 29 minutes. However, because there were other world-class runners at the race, he decided that he should stay with the pack from the start. After a proper warm-up, he did just that, but not without consequences. Because he was wearing his pulse monitor, he was able to keep tabs on heart rate and pace. The first mile was very fast, and his pulse quickly jumped above 180 bpm. After the first mile, he knew that he would have to fight just to hang on to the pack. Each mile after the first, his time per mile increased by about 10 seconds. He completed the race 2½ minutes behind the leader. An explanation of what happened is that he was racing above his AT for the first mile, and his body could not deal with the metabolic strain of running that fast. If he had run at his known AT pace, he might have held on to a slightly faster average pace for the entire race, finishing better than he actually did.

You may be asking, "How do I find my own AT pace or heart rate?" Subjectively, you can focus on how your legs and arms feel, the rhythm of your breathing, and your overall bodily feeling when doing Intervals or Race/Pace workouts. Try to distinguish the feelings of staying within the aerobic zone and going beyond it into anaerobic exercise. Another method is to use the Test Conconi, as many cyclists, skiers, and runners are doing, to determine your AT heart rate and pace. The Test Conconi will give you objective information regarding heart rate and pace at AT, as well as all the subjective physiological and psychological cues that indicate you are at threshold.

The Test Conconi for Runners, Skiers, and Triathletes

CAUTION: Make sure you are in good health before you try this test

Necessary Equipment

You'll need a reliable heart monitor (preferably one that uses a chest strap transmitter and wristwatch receiver, because these are extremely reliable and accurate) and two assistants—one equipped with a stopwatch, a notebook, several copies of Worksheet E.1, and a pencil; the second equipped with a bicycle set up with a cycle computer that reads out speed in kilometers per hour (mph is okay if that's all you've got). Find a 200-meter indoor track with a surface smooth enough for a cyclist to ride comfortably (outdoor tracks may be used, but then wind is a variable, and you'll have to do the test on a completely windless day).

First, measure and mark one section of track 50 meters in length (for a 400-meter track, mark two 50-meter sections exactly 200 meters apart). I use cones or flags to mark the beginning and end of each 50-meter section so that the assistant can see them from the middle of the infield of the track.

Starting the Test

You'll be running behind the bicycling assistant around the track for each lap, so the cyclist must maintain even speed throughout each lap. Speed will be increased by ½ kilometer per hour every 200-meter lap. After a proper 20- to 30-minute warm-up, start the test by following the cyclist at a pace that is comfortable and at a Level II intensity heart rate.

After each 200-meter lap (marked by the second cone in the 50-meter section), the cyclist increases the pace by ½ kilometer per hour and maintains the new pace for the entire lap. (If you are doing the test without the assistance of a cyclist pacer, increase your running speed by about 5 seconds per kilometer).

Your second assistant must time the final 50 meters of each 200-meter section so that your actual running speed in kilometers per hour can be determined. If you feel that the cycle computer is accurate and that you are staying an even distance behind the bike, you can simply record the speed indicated by the cycle computer, which the cyclist can give to the recording assistant after each lap. Each time you pass the end of the marked 50 meters, call out your heart rate. Your assistant will record that figure next to the time for that 50-meter section. Continue this pattern until you feel that you have passed the AT and you feel that your heart rate is no longer increasing as fast as your speed. You'll be running quite fast at that point.

The Conconi Test for Cyclists

Necessary Equipment

As in the running test, you'll need a heart rate monitor and an assistant. You'll also need a bike computer that measures speed and cadence. Ideally, the test is performed on a velodrome, but you can use a wind trainer to do the test indoors.

Starting the Test

After warming up for 15 to 30 minutes, start riding the first of 10 to 15 laps or intervals. Each lap should measure between 300 and 450 meters. If you are using a wind trainer, use an appropriate time for each interval (between 30 to 50 seconds per 400 meters). You need to use a moderately large gear for the duration of the test. Be sure to ride in the racing position. Maintain a constant pace during each lap. (Begin at 10 mph or less if you are a beginner.) Increase your speed by 1 mph for each lap until the fatigue and burning in your legs makes it impossible to continue. As you pass your assistant at the end of each lap, call out your heart rate so it can be recorded.

Calculating the AT

Now come the data analysis and calculation of your AT. Calculate your running speed from the time per 50-meter section (if you cycled, you already know the speed for each lap). On the graph in Worksheet E.1, plot your heart rate on the vertical axis and your speed on the horizontal axis. Theoretically, if the test went as planned, your graph should show an evenly sloping line—until the point where your heart rate does not increase linearly relative to your speed. The speed at that point, as indicated by the "knee" in the graph, is where you reached your AT, as illustrated in Figure E.1. Conconi calls this point the V_d (velocity of deflection) and considers the heart rate and speed at this point to be the AT.

Interpreting the AT

Now that you know your AT, what do you do with it? Every SERIOUS training plan incorporates Level IV intensity or AT training in a systematic manner. Each Interval, Vertical, and Race/Pace workout should be accomplished at 5 to 10 beats per minute below the AT heart rate. Over the course of the training plan, you should gradually increase the percentage of AT training. In theory, the AT itself will increase, occurring at a higher percentage of your VO_2max, and your VO_2max will also rise. Your Race/Pace at threshold will also improve, enabling you to cover the same distance in less time at the same intensity.

A word to the wise about the Test Conconi (I've experienced a few glitches in using this test). First, if you're running on a track with a strong headwind on one side, your graph will come out looking rather uneven. Second, be sure that the increase in speed with each 200 meters is systematic—that's why running behind a cyclist with a cycle computer is so helpful. If you are pacing yourself, increase your speed ever so slightly, and consistently between laps. Third, be sure that your assistant starts and stops the clock precisely when you cross the marks at the beginning and end of the 50-meter section. Otherwise, you may get inaccurate times. The ideal place to do this test is at an indoor track.

Testing Frequency

How often should you take the Test Conconi? If logistically feasible, you can use the test every 2 to 4 weeks to check your AT during the Intensity Stage. If everything is going according to theory and plan, your AT will increase gradually, and you'll be able to use each new AT heart rate and pace to train for Intervals, Vertical, and Race/Pace.

WORKSHEET E.1:
Data Sheet For Recording Heart Rate and Speed For Test Conconi

Name   Date

Loop #	Heart rate	Time (sec/50 m)	Speed (km/hr)
1			
2			
3			
4			
5			
6			
7			
8			
9			
10			
11			
12			
13			
14			
15			
16			
17			
18			

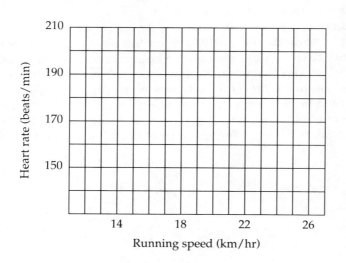

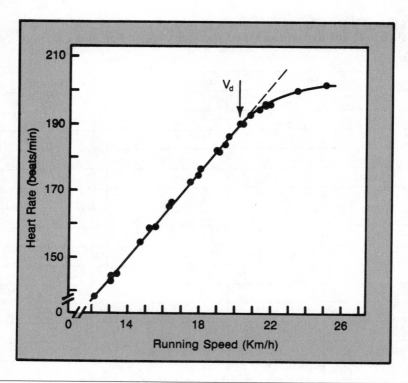

Figure E.1 Heart rate and speed for Test Conconi.

If your AT pace and heart rate decrease, it could be a sign of over-training. Before jumping to conclusions, look at your training log to monitor all the other stress symptoms.

Although the Test Conconi may be useful to many, much controversy surrounds the test and even the very notion of anaerobic threshold. Exercise physiologists are bound to continue their research and produce new arguments about this subject. Meanwhile, I encourage you to try the Test Conconi—or at least tune in to your AT feelings when you train. In any case, remember that the essential aspect of Level IV training is that you are training hard enough but not so hard that your exercise quickly becomes anaerobic.

REFERENCES

Anderson, R. (1980). *Stretching*. Bolinas, CA: Shelter Publications.

Asmussen, E., & Boje, O. (1960). Body temperature and capacity for work. *Acta Physiologica Scandinavica*, **49**, 67.

Åstrand, P.O., & Rodahl, K. (1977). *Textbook of work physiology*. New York: McGraw-Hill.

Barnard, R.J. (1973). Ischemic response to sudden strenuous exercise in healthy men. *Circulation*, **158**, 936-942.

Bergstrom, J., Hermansen, L., Hultman, E., & Saltin, B. (1967). Diet, muscle glycogen and physical performance. *Acta Physiologica Scandinavica*, **71**, 140-150.

Blom, P., Vaage, O., & Kardel, K. (1980). The effect of increasing glucose loads on the rate of glycogen resynthesis after prolonged exercise. *Acta Physiologica Scandinavica*, **108**, C11.

Conconi, F., Ferrari, M., Ziglio, P.G., Droghetti, P., & Codeca, L. (1982). Determination of the anaerobic threshold by a noninvasive field test in runners. *Journal of Applied Physiology*, **52**, 869-873.

Costill, D.L. (1979). *A scientific approach to distance running*. Los Altos, CA: Track and Field News Press.

deVries, H.A. (1959). Effects of various warm up procedures on 100-yard times of competitive swimmers. *Research Quarterly*, **30**, 11-20.

Ellsworth, N.A., Hewitt, B.F., & Haskell, W.L. (1985). Nutrient intake of elite male and female Nordic skiers. *The Physician and Sportsmedicine*, **13**, 79-92.

Fink, W. (1982). Fluid intake for maximizing athletic performance. In W. Haskell (Ed.), *Nutrition and Athletic Performance* (p. 76). Palo Alto, CA: Bull.

Gollnick, P.D. (1985). Metabolism of substrates: Energy substrate metabolism during exercise and as modified by training. *Federation Proceedings*, **44**, 353-357.

Hogberg, P., & Ljunggren, O. (1947). Uppvarmningens inverkan pa lopprestationerna, *Svensk Idrott*, **40**.

Holloszy, J., & Booth, F. (1976). Biochemical adaptations to endurance exercise in muscle. *Annual Review of Physiology*, **38**, 273.

Karvonen, J. (1978). *Warming up and its physiological effects*. Unpublished doctoral dissertation, University of Oulu, Finland.

Koivisto, V., Hendler, R., & Nadel, E. (1982). Influence of physical training on the fuel-hormone response to prolonged low intensity exercise. *Metabolism, 31,* 192.

Macaraeg, P. (1983). Influence of carbohydrate electrolyte ingestion on running endurance. In E.L. Fox (Ed.), *Nutrient utilization during exercise,* (pp. 91-98). Columbus, OH: Ross Laboratories.

Orlick, T. (1986). *Psyching for sport.* Champaign, IL: Leisure Press.

Robinson, S. (1963). Temperature regulation in exercise. *Pediatrics, 32,* 691-702.

Shevciw, T. (1986, February). Regeneration alternatives in high performance sport. *Science Periodical on Research and Technology in Sport,* 1-8.

Sharkey, B.J. (1984). *Training for cross-country ski racing.* Champaign, IL: Human Kinetics.

Sherman, W.M., Costill, D.L., Fink, W.J., & Miller, J.M. (1981). Effects of exercise-diet manipulation on muscle glycogen and its subsequent utilization during performance. *International Journal of Sports Medicine, 2,* 1-15.

Yessis, M. (1986, July). Recovery. *Science Periodical on Research and Technology in Sport, 2.*

RECOMMENDED READING

Åstrand, P.O., & Rodahl, K. (1977). *Textbook of work physiology*. New York: McGraw-Hill.

Bergh, U. (1981). *The physiology of cross-country ski racing*. Champaign, IL: Human Kinetics.

Brody, J. (1981). *Jane Brody's nutrition book*. New York: W.W. Norton.

Brody, J. (1985). *Jane Brody's good food book*. New York: W.W. Norton.

Costill, D.L. (1979). *A scientific approach to distance running*. Los Altos, CA: Track and Field News Press.

Orlick, T. (1986). *Psyching for sport*. Champaign, IL: Leisure Press.

Phaigh, R., & Perry, P. (1984). *Athletic massage*. New York: Simon and Schuster.

Sharkey, B. (1984). *Physiology of fitness*. Champaign, IL: Human Kinetics.

Sharkey, B. (1984). *Training for cross-country ski racing*. Champaign, IL: Human Kinetics.

Wilmore, J.H. (1982). *Athletic training and physical fitness*. Boston: Allyn and Bacon.

INDEX

Numbers in italics refer to figures.

ABOUT THE AUTHOR

Rob Sleamaker has devoted most of his career to studying the scientific principles of endurance training and applying those principles to his work with elite and recreational athletes. Since earning his master's degree in exercise physiology from the University of Arizona, Rob has fulfilled a variety of sport-related responsibilities. He has worked as a sport physiologist at a sports medicine clinic in Burlington, Vermont, and assisted in research on the effects of exercise during pregnancy at the University of Vermont. From 1984 to 1986,  Rob was director of sports medicine for the U.S. Biathlon Team. Since 1986, he has run his own business, Compufit, which provides personalized sport and fitness training systems to individuals as well as computer software for the fitness industry. Rob is a constant innovator and inventor, most recently developing the Väsa Trainer, a sports-specific strength/endurance exerciser.

Rob frequently authors feature articles on endurance-sport training for major sport and fitness magazines, and he continues to coach several athletes. He lives in a log home in Williston, Vermont, with a cross-country ski center only a few feet from his front door. An avid cross-country ski racer and biathlete, Rob also enjoys running, mountain biking, hiking, canoeing, reading, writing, and spending time in the wilderness.

SERIOUS Training for Serious Athletes contains all the information you need to prepare your own personalized training program. However, if you would like more information about having Rob Sleamaker create a training plan for you, contact COMPUFIT, Attn. Rob Sleamaker, 372 Governor Chittenden Road, Williston, VT 05495.